without the calories | slow cooker

Justine Pattison

contents

introduction 5

slow cooking briefly explained 8

chicken 12

lamb 38

beef 54

pork and ham 74

meat-free 94

fish and seafood 114

sweet things 126

other things 148

a few notes on the recipes 172

essential extras 176

simple snacks 178

nutritional information 180

index 186

introduction

MY STORY

I struggled with my weight for years. After being a skinny child and teenager, I piled on the weight during my last years of school and went into my twenties feeling fat and frumpy. A career as a cookery writer and food stylist has helped me understand good food but because my kitchen is always overflowing with great things to eat, temptation is never far away. My weight yo-yoed for twenty years and at my heaviest I weighed more than 15 stone.

A few years ago, I worked on the hit TV series *You Are What You Eat* – I put together those groaning tables of bad food. I also had the chance to work with the contributors on the show, guiding them through the dieting process and helping them discover a whole new way of eating and cooking. Having been overweight myself, I became passionate about helping people lose weight.

Since then, I've worked as a food consultant on many of the weight-loss shows you've seen on TV, and written diet plans and recipes for best-selling books, newspapers and magazines. I'm thrilled that thousands of people have successfully followed my way of cooking and lost weight.

This book, and the others in the series, are ideal for anyone who wants to lose weight while leading a normal life. Cooking my way will help you sustain a happy, healthy weight loss. That's what it's all about: you don't have to be stick thin, but you deserve to feel good about yourself. My recipes will help you reach your goal.

ABOUT THIS BOOK

From the feedback I've been given, I know that lots of you love your electric slow cooker, but have had trouble finding healthy recipes that taste good too. So I set myself the task of creating the best possible book to satisfy that need and in doing so I've learnt more about slow cooking than I thought possible.

For instance, the variety of meals you can prepare in a slow cooker is enormous – everything from succulent pulled pork, to a hearty casserole, quiche, light sponge puddings, crème caramel and even yoghurt. What's more, it's particularly useful for those of us watching our weight as food can be cooked in bulk and frozen in handy portions, or quickly prepared on a busy day, meaning there is always a healthy choice available.

As with the other books in the *Without the Calories* series, I've reworked ingredients to reduce as many calories as possible, while still trying hard to keep all the flavour and appetite appeal, helping you lose weight in the most delicious and simple way.

I'm not going to make rash promises about how many pounds you will shed, but I do know that when it comes to losing weight, finding foods that give you pleasure and fit into your lifestyle are the key to success. When you eat well without obsessing over rapid weight loss, it's easier to relax and lose what you need to comfortably – and safely.

To help everyone enjoy these reinvented dishes, I've used easy-to-find ingredients and given clear, simple cooking instructions. There's also freezer information included where appropriate, so you know which dishes you can store safely for another day.

If you're already following a diet plan, you'll find additional nutritional information

USING THE WTC PLAN

If you're not following a diet regime at the moment and want a great kick-start, try my WTC Plan for a few weeks. I've tried to make it really easy, and you don't need to do too much adding-up. You'll find more than 500 recipes to choose from in the *Without the Calories* series. Simply pick recipes that bring your daily intake to between 900 and 1,200 calories. Add large portions of vegetables or salad, plus an essential extra 300 calories a day, and you'll be on your way to a healthy, sustainable weight loss of between 2–3lb a week.

I've colour coded all the calorie calculations at the top of each recipe, so you can quickly make your choice as you flick through the book. You will also find a selection of desserts and cakes in this book. Although they are lower in fat, sugar and calories than traditional recipes, it's best not to eat them every day, but to enjoy them every now and then as part of your total calorie allowance. For this reason, they have their own category: *Occasional Extras* (calories printed in green).

ONE
up to 300 calories

TWO
300–400 calories

THREE
400–550 calories

*Occasional Extras

If you want to add your own favourite meals into the plan, simply make sure they are within the recommended calorie boundaries and calculate accordingly. (You may find this useful when planning breakfast especially.)

YOUR ESSENTIAL EXTRAS

Your essential extra 300 calories can be made up of accompaniments such as potatoes, rice and pasta, as well as snacks or treats; there are suggestions and serving sizes on page 176. I've also put together a list of foods that can be eaten as simple snacks on page 178.

at the back of the book that'll help you work my recipes into your week. And, if you're stuck for inspiration and have a few pounds to lose, try my WTC Plan (see above). It couldn't be easier.

DON'T RUSH IT

Weight tends to be gained over time, and losing it gradually will make the process easier and help give your body, especially your skin, time to adapt. You're more likely to get into positive, enjoyable long-term cooking and eating habits this way too.

WHAT IS A CALORIE?

Put simply, a calorie is a unit of energy contained within food and drink which our

bodies burn as fuel. Different foods contain varying amounts of calories, and if more calories are consumed than the body needs, the excess will be stored as fat. To lose weight, we need to eat less or use more energy by increasing our activity – and ideally both!

I've provided the calorie content of a single serving of each dish. In my experience, most people will lose at least 2lb a week by consuming around 1,200–1,500 calories a day, but it's always best to check with your GP before you start a new regime. Everyone is different and, especially if you have several stone to lose, you'll need some personalised advice. The calories contained in each recipe have been calculated as accurately as possible, but could vary a little depending on your ingredients.

If you have a couple of days of eating more than 1,400 calories, try to eat closer to 1,100 for the next few days. Over a week, things will even out.

My recipes strike a balance between eating and cooking well and reducing calories, and I've tried them all as part of my own way of enjoying food without putting on excess weight. Even if you don't need to lose weight, I hope you enjoy cooking from my books simply because you like the recipes.

SECRETS OF SUCCESS

The serving sizes that I've recommended form the basis of the nutritional information on page 180, and if you eat any more, you may find losing weight takes longer. If you're cooking for anyone who doesn't need to watch their calorie intake, you can increase their servings, but bear in mind that too much sugar isn't good for anyone.

The right portion size also holds the key to maintaining your weight loss. Use this opportunity to get used to smaller servings. Work out exactly how much food your body needs to maintain the shape that makes you feel great. That way, even when counting calories feels like a distant memory, you'll remain in control of your eating habits.

Stick to lean protein (which will help you feel fuller for longer) and vegetables and avoid high-fat, high-sugar snacks and confectionery. Be aware that alcohol is packed with empty calories and could weaken your resolve. Starchy carbs such as pasta, rice, potatoes and bread are kept to a minimum because I've found that, combined with eating lots of veg and good protein, this leads to more sustainable weight loss. There's no need to avoid dairy products such as cheese and cream, although they tend to be high in fat and calories. You can swap the high-fat versions for reduced-fat ones, or use less.

Ditch heavily processed foods and you will feel so much better. Switching to more natural ingredients will help your body work with you.

Most recipes in the series form the main part of a meal, so there's room to have your plate half-filled with freshly cooked vegetables or a colourful, crunchy salad. This will help fill you up, and boost your intake of fibre, vitamins and minerals.

Make sure you drink enough fluids, especially water – about 2 litres is ideal. Staying hydrated will help you lose weight more comfortably, and it's important when you exercise, too.

IN THE KITCHEN

Pick up some electronic kitchen scales and a set of measuring spoons if you don't already have them. Both will probably cost less than a takeaway meal for two, and will help ensure good results.

Invest, if you can, in a large, deep non-stick frying pan, a medium non-stick saucepan and a large saucepan for extra vegetables, rice, pasta and potatoes. The non-stick coating means that you will need less oil to cook, and a frying pan with a wide base and deep sides can double as a wok.

STICK WITH IT

Shifting your eating habits and trying to lose weight is not easy, especially if you have been eating the same way for many years. But it isn't too late. You may never have the perfect body, but you can have one that, fuelled by really good food, makes you feel happy and healthy. For more information, tips and ideas, visit www.justinepattison.co.uk. And for extra weight loss support, join my free group www.facebook.com/groups/JustinePattison.

slow cooking briefly explained

For me, slow cooking isn't just about food you put in the slow cooker first thing in the morning and then eat 12 hours later. In fact, not many foods can stand being cooked for that length of time. I like the flexibility of being able to switch between cooking for a long and a shorter time depending on the day.

It's just as useful to put a meal in the slow cooker mid-morning, and for it to be ready 6–7 hours later, as it is to throw together something that might take just 2–3 hours. All the recipes in this book have been tested at a HIGH and a LOW setting. By giving both temperatures, I hope you get the kind of flexibility you need to suit your life.

Ultimately, slow cooking isn't an exact science and it can take a little while to get to know your own slow cooker. Look carefully at the manufacturer's instructions for detailed information and guidance. If you start checking your food close to the shortest time I've recommended, you shouldn't be too far off.

It seems that older slow cookers generally cook at a lower temperature than the more modern ones, so do check your food at the shorter times I have given, but remember it might need longer depending on the model and will need to reach a safe eating temperature.

How does a slow cooker work?
Most slow cookers have a removable pot insert within a metal casing that holds an electric element. The element surrounds the pot and heats it from the base and sides.

How do I choose the right slow cooker?
Firstly, it depends on how many people you need to feed, or whether you fancy cooking food in bulk and then freezing for another day – which is brilliant for the health-conscious cook. Different sized slow cookers have different capacities. As a rule of thumb, I work to the following:

2.5-litre capacity – serves 2–3 people
3.5-litre capacity – serves 3–5 people
4.5-litre capacity – serves 4–6 people
6.5-litre capacity – serves 6–8 people

I've found during the testing of the recipes in this book – when I have been using 12 different slow cookers – size does matter, but not as much as you might think. You may not be able to cook a recipe designed for six people in a 2.5-litre slow cooker, but you could cook a couple of chicken breasts in a 4.5-litre slow cooker without ruining them. You just need to keep an eye on timings. If you are cooking a small quantity in a large slow cooker, you may need to reduce the cooking time, and if you are cooking a large quantity in a small slow cooker, it is likely to take a bit longer.

The majority of slow cookers have a removable ceramic or metal insert, sometimes called a crockpot or slow cooker dish. For the purposes of this book, I've called it a pot. It's best to buy a slow cooker that has a removable pot, because it makes the slow cooker easier to clean. The pot itself can be immersed in water and some even go in the dishwasher. It's also best to choose a slow cooker with a glass lid, so you can see, to some extent, what's going on. And always choose a cooker with an indicator light, so you know it is turned on.

Are thick ceramic pots or the metal kind you can use on the hob best?
I've used both types and I think it depends on what your needs are. The thick ceramic pots heat slowly but evenly and I think they cook food more gently, so they are great for all-day stews and large pieces of meat. They also hold

the heat better and look more attractive if taken to the table.

The metal kind can be used on the hob for browning meat and vegetables, which is handy for smaller amounts. (I find a large non-stick frying pan just as useful, although it does create extra washing up.) If you want to cook your food at a faster rate, the metal inserts heat more rapidly too, so food will reach a suitable cooking temperature fairly speedily; great if you want to bung something on for just a couple of hours or so. The metal inserts are easier to wash and considerably lighter to carry.

What do the different settings on the slow cooker mean?

You'll probably find that your slow cooker has a HIGH and a LOW setting, with perhaps a MEDIUM or AUTO setting too. HIGH and LOW settings are likely to bring food to the same temperature, but with the LOW setting it will take longer to get there. The MEDIUM setting is somewhere in between and the AUTO setting starts off HIGH to get the food going and will switch to LOW after an hour or so. A digital display is really useful as it has a timer that counts down the minutes (usually in half-hour increments) and then switches to WARM once the food is cooked. The WARM setting can keep food at a safe temperature for up to 2 hours (depending on the manufacturer and model) but should not be used for cooking.

How much food should I put in the slow cooker?

Most manufacturers recommend that the slow cooker is never less than half full and no more than three-quarters full. The quantity of food in the slow cooker will affect the cooking time. If there is too little, the food could dry out, and if there is too much, there is a risk that hot liquid could bubble out from the lid. Too much food in the cooker can result in uneven cooking too, with the food closest to the base and sides cooking more quickly than the food in the middle. If you are adding liquid, make sure it doesn't rise more than about halfway up the sides as there will be very little evaporation, so you need less than usual. Ideally, choose recipes close to the serving sizes recommended for your slow cooker, or adapt timings if necessary.

Is slow cooking best for cheaper cuts of meat?

Slow cooking is perfect for tenderising cheaper, tougher cuts of meat. If you are worried about using fattier cuts, don't be; the fat adds lots of flavour and current nutritional thinking promotes low-sugar rather than low-fat eating. Simply cut off any hard areas of fat you can easily reach and don't worry about the rest.

What will happen if I use leaner cuts in the slow cooker?

If you wish to switch to a leaner cut (such as swapping lamb neck for leg meat), be aware that the meat will still be tender after a long cook but it will be a little less succulent. But don't worry as long as you have lots of flavoursome sauce and some good vegetables.

Can I cook chicken breasts in the slow cooker?

Some books say no, but I've included a few chicken breast recipes here as they are more popular than thighs. The cheaper chicken breasts stand up to slow cooking best, with the firm, dense free-range chicken drying out more quickly. Just keep an eye on the cooking times and switch to boneless, skinless thighs if you want to cook your chicken for longer than 2–3 hours.

Do I need to brown food on the hob before adding it to the slow cooker?

Several of the dishes in this book require meat, poultry, onions and some aromatics, such as garlic, ginger or spices, to be quickly fried before they are added to the slow cooker.

I found that this simple step adds a depth of flavour to casseroles and curries that really improves the final results, but you can bung everything in together without browning it if you are short of time. (Add 2–3 teaspoons of Marmite to the pot at the beginning of the cooking time and you'll help give the dish a richer flavour and colour when you don't have time to brown it first.) Remember to increase the cooking time if not pre-browning. Some meats, especially chicken and pork, look far more appetising if they are browned first, but remember you will be adding a few calories with the oil.

Can I prepare the dishes in advance?

Yes, absolutely. If you want to get ahead, prepare your slow cooker dish the night before (without any liquid), and put it in a freezer bag, or bowl, in the fridge. Add it to the slow cooker pot in the morning, along with the liquid. If you have browned any vegetables, make sure they are completely cold before adding them to the rest of the ingredients and putting them in the fridge. Do not brown or part cook meat and poultry in advance as it could result in food safety issues. Again, check the manufacturer's instructions. Because all the ingredients have been chilled, you can expect some dishes to take longer to cook (which could be handy if you are out all day).

Should I preheat my slow cooker?

If you have a slow cooker with a metal pot insert it can probably be preheated, but ceramic pots often shouldn't be heated when empty. One way around this is to half-fill the pot with warm water and preheat it for 15 minutes or so, then carefully throw away the water and fill it with your ingredients.

I've read that lifting the lid adds about half an hour to the cooking time. Is this true?

I would say that it's best not to lift the lid until the food has reached a good cooking temperature – probably after about 2 hours on HIGH or 4 hours on LOW. And then only lift off if absolutely necessary. If you are adding another ingredient, want to check ingredients are cooked, or think the food would benefit from stirring, replace the lid as quickly as possible to maintain the temperature inside the cooker and reduce the amount of evaporation.

Why do I need to add water to the slow cooker when I'm cooking certain dishes?

Adding water to the slow cooker slows down the cooking process and helps delicate foods cook more gently, so there is less risk of curdling or overcooking. Make sure the food is in covered containers, such as bowls or ramekins topped with foil, so water doesn't drop in from the lid. Place in the slow cooker and pour water around them, rising to about halfway up the sides.

Can I freeze food cooked in my slow cooker?

Yes, definitely. Ideally, cook the food for a little less than usual, depending on cooking time, so it is safely cooked but isn't too soft before cooling and freezing. Freezing and reheating will soften it further. But, if you want to freeze leftovers, don't worry too much, just freeze in small portions so it can be reheated as quickly as possible, ideally in a microwave so it doesn't need to be stirred too much (which could break up the pieces). (See the freezer tips on page 173.) I've given freezing instructions for all the recipes suitable for freezing.

Can I leave food to cool in the slow cooker?

No, that's not recommended. Once it has finished cooking, or had about 2 hours on the WARM setting (check the manufacturer's instructions), it is best to remove the pot insert and either serve or transfer the food to another dish to cool down quickly. You should also never reheat cooked food in the slow cooker.

Can I put frozen food in the slow cooker?

No, that's not recommended. Frozen food takes too long to thaw and then heat, meaning it might not reach a safe enough temperature to eat when you need it.

Special equipment

You don't really need any special equipment for your slow cooker as most things are cooked in the pot itself. The main exceptions to this are the following kit:

Foil loaf tins

These are the type of tins used for takeaways and freezing – you can pick them up cheaply in most supermarkets, pound stores and online. I use these tins to make quiche-style dishes that would overcook in direct contact with the slow cooker. I use the 450g size, which fits nicely into most slow cookers. You will need to line it with baking parchment, to stop anything sticking. I buy the disposable cake tin liners (but you could cut up a silicone lining sheet to fit). I also put the filled tin on a couple of upturned ramekins, to help raise it enough to fit properly in the slow cooker.

Mini metal pudding basins and ramekins

These are widely available and perfect for individual puddings, such as crème caramel (see page 134). They will need to hold 175–200ml for the recipes in this book.

Baking parchment

I use baking parchment to line the slow cooker pot when cooking cakes and puddings, and for creating a barrier to condensation when cooking potatoes.

Digital thermometer

As always, it's well worth investing in a digital food thermometer. A well-made thermometer will last for many years and remove all the uncertainty when checking whether food is safely cooked. As well as taking the core temperature of stews and curries, the thermometer will make sure that denser meats, such as gammon, are cooked correctly, so there is far less chance that they will be spoilt.

chicken

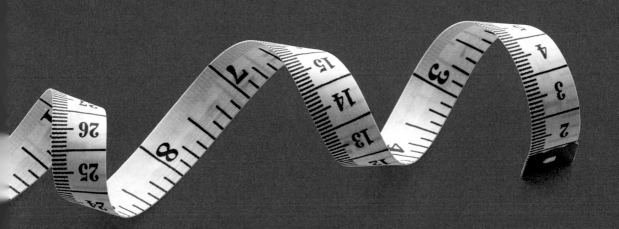

213
CALORIES
PER SERVING

slow-roast chicken

SERVES 5
PREP: 10-12 MINUTES
HIGH 4-5 HOURS

1.6kg whole chicken
1 tsp flaked sea salt
1 tsp ground black pepper
2 tsp oil
2-3 bushy thyme sprigs
   (optional)

Tip: Check the manufacturer's instructions to make sure that you can preheat and cook a whole chicken in your slow cooker.

Chicken cooked very slowly is incredibly moist and delicious. Serve hot with vegetables or allow to cool and use for sandwiches and salads. There is no need to brown it first, but I always think this makes the chicken look far more appetising. Simply leave out that stage if you are running out of time. (The calories have been calculated for cooked chicken without the skin.)

Preheat your slow cooker on HIGH. Remove any trussing string from the chicken and season the bird all over with the salt and pepper.

Heat the oil in a large non-stick frying pan and brown the chicken for 8-10 minutes, turning it every now and then until golden brown all over. Take care as you turn the chicken – I use a couple of long forks or tongs. Pop the thyme sprigs into the body cavity if you like.

Place the chicken in the slow cooker, breast side up. Cover with the lid and cook on HIGH for 4-5 hours or until tender and thoroughly cooked – the meat should be almost falling off the bones. Remove the lid and test with a digital thermometer or pierce the thickest part of the bird with a skewer and make sure the juices run clear. If you wiggle one of the legs, it should move very easily.

Transfer the chicken carefully to a board and carve into chunky pieces to serve.

Quick gravy: Take the chicken out of the slow cooker and strain the cooking juices through a sieve into a small pan. You should have about 140ml of cooking liquor. Add 3 tablespoons of white wine, 1 rasher of smoked back bacon, 1 tablespoon of redcurrant jelly, 1 teaspoon of Marmite and 250ml chicken stock, made with half a chicken stock cube. Bring to a simmer and cook for 3-4 minutes, stirring regularly. Blend 1 tablespoon of cornflour with 1 tablespoon of cold water to form a smooth paste and stir it into the gravy, then continue to cook for a further 2-3 minutes, stirring. Remove the bacon and adjust the seasoning to taste. Serves 5. Calories per serving: 38

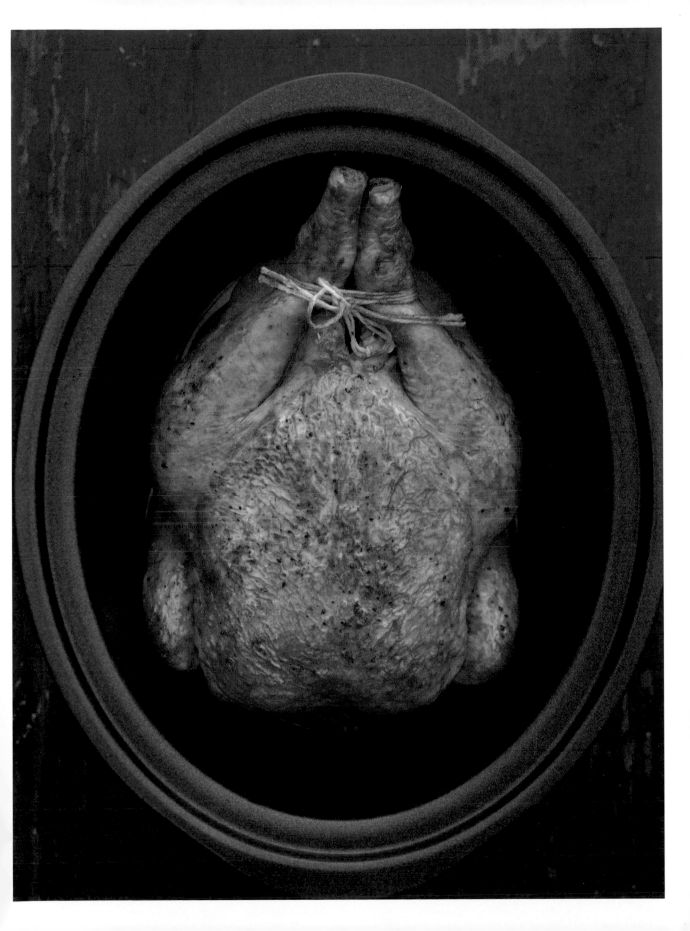

241
CALORIES
PER SERVING

easy italian chicken

1 tsp oil

4 boneless, skinless chicken breasts (each about 150g)

500g jar of tomato pasta sauce, or home-made

65g pitted mixed green and black olives, drained

¼–½ tsp dried chilli flakes (optional)

flaked sea salt

ground black pepper

Tip: A block of Parmesan is expensive, but a little goes a long way and it will make this simple chicken dish taste extra-special. Sprinkle a little grated Parmesan over the chicken just before serving. Don't forget to add an extra 50 calories for every 10g you use. Wrap the block in foil and keep in the fridge once opened. It will last for several weeks.

If you are using unpitted olives, increase the quantity to 100g, and don't forget to warn people about the stones!

This recipe really couldn't be simpler. You can use a shop-bought jar of tomato pasta sauce – the ones for Bolognese are good here. You can also use a home-made tomato sauce – see the recipe on page 166. Add a few olives and a pinch of chilli if you like. If you want a chicken dish that can be left cooking for longer, swap the breasts for eight boneless, skinless thighs and they should cook for six hours on LOW without drying out.

Heat the oil in a large non-stick frying pan. Season the chicken breasts with salt and pepper and fry them over a medium-high heat for 2–3 minutes on each side, or until lightly browned.

Pour the tomato sauce into the slow cooker and add the olives and chilli flakes (if using). Place the chicken breasts on top. Cover with the lid and cook on HIGH for 2–3 hours, or until the chicken is thoroughly cooked and perfectly tender.

Serve with a small portion of freshly cooked pasta or new potatoes and a large mixed salad.

449
CALORIES
PER SERVING

coronation chicken

SERVES 6

**PREP: 30 MINUTES,
PLUS CHILLING TIME**

HIGH 4-5 HOURS

1.6kg whole chicken

FOR THE SAUCE
1 medium onion
1 tbsp oil
4 tsp medium curry powder
3 tbsp tomato purée
2 tbsp mango chutney
200ml chicken stock
   (made with ½ chicken
   stock cube)
150g mayonnaise
200g full-fat plain bio
   yoghurt
50g sultanas
25g bunch of fresh
   coriander (optional)
25g rocket leaves (optional)
10g toasted flaked almonds
flaked sea salt
ground black pepper

Tip: Check the manufacturer's
instructions to make sure
that you can preheat and
cook a whole chicken in
your slow cooker.

**Chicken poached gently in a slow cooker is guaranteed
to be deliciously tender and moist. Coronation chicken makes
a great dish for a party and can be prepared a day ahead.
Use any leftovers for sandwiches and wraps.**

Preheat your slow cooker. Remove any trussing string from the
chicken. Place the chicken in the slow cooker, breast side up.
Cover with the lid and cook on HIGH for 4-5 hours, or until
tender and completely cooked. Test with a digital thermometer
or pierce the thickest part of the bird with a skewer and make
sure the juices run clear. If you wiggle one of the legs, it should
move very easily. Transfer the chicken carefully to a board and
leave to cool for 30 minutes. Reserve the cooking liquor.

To make the sauce, peel and very finely chop the onion. Heat
the oil in a medium non-stick saucepan and add the onion.
Cook over a medium heat for 3-5 minutes, stirring occasionally.

Add the curry powder and cook for a further minute, stirring
continuously (do not allow it to burn). Stir in the tomato purée
and mango chutney and cook for 30 seconds more, stirring,
then add the reserved cooking liquor and stock and bring to a
simmer. Cook for 8-10 minutes, or until the liquid is reduced
and the onion mixture looks thickened and sauce-like. Transfer
to a mixing bowl and leave to cool.

Remove the chicken skin and strip the meat from the bones.
Cut the meat into bite-sized pieces, put on a plate, cover and
place in the fridge until the sauce is ready. (Discard the chicken
skin and bones.)

Once the curried onions are cold, stir in the mayonnaise, yoghurt
and sultanas. Finely chop the coriander, if using, reserving a few
sprigs for garnish. Stir the chopped coriander into the sauce and
adjust the seasoning with salt and pepper to taste.

Mix the cold sauce with the chilled chicken, cover and return
to the fridge for at least 1 hour before serving. When ready to
serve, toss with the rocket leaves, if using, and spoon on to a
serving platter. Garnish with flaked almonds and coriander.

305

CALORIES
PER SERVING

chinese chicken

SERVES 4

PREP: 20 MINUTES

**HIGH 2-3 HOURS,
PLUS 20 MINUTES**

500g boneless, skinless
  chicken breasts
1 medium onion
2 tsp oil
425g can pineapple slices in
  natural juice
1 red, 1 green and 1 yellow
  pepper
25g chunk of fresh root
  ginger
2 garlic cloves
225g can water chestnuts
  (optional)
3 tbsp cornflour
2 tbsp dark soy sauce
2 tbsp tomato ketchup
2 tbsp soft light brown
  sugar
2 tbsp white wine vinegar
ground black pepper
2 spring onions, to garnish
  (optional)

Home-made sweet and sour chicken beats using a jar or
heading out for a takeaway, and is far less sickly. Water
chestnuts are not nuts at all but aquatic vegetables. They have
a great crisp texture and add a lovely crunch to this dish. For a
slower cooked dish, use boneless, skinless chicken thighs
instead of breasts and cook on LOW for 4-5 hours.

Cut the chicken breasts into roughly 3cm chunks and season
with black pepper. Peel and cut the onion into thin wedges.
Heat the oil in a large non-stick frying pan or wok and stir-fry
the chicken and onion over a high heat for 2-3 minutes, or until
just cooked and lightly browned.

Drain the pineapple through a sieve over a bowl and reserve all
the juice. Cut the pineapple into chunks and put to one side.
Deseed all the peppers and cut into roughly 3cm chunks, peel
and cut the ginger and garlic into very thin slices, and drain and
halve the water chestnuts (if using).

Put the cornflour in a medium bowl and stir in 3 tablespoons
of the pineapple juice to make a smooth paste. Pour the rest of
the pineapple juice into the slow cooker, add the soy sauce,
ketchup, sugar and vinegar and stir until combined.

Add the chicken, onion, ginger, garlic and water chestnuts (if
using) and mix, then place the peppers on top. Cover with the
lid and cook on HIGH for 2-3 hours, or until the chicken is
thoroughly cooked and the sauce is bubbling. Remove the lid
and add the pineapple pieces. Stir the cornflour mixture and
add it to the slow cooker. Combine well.

Cover again and cook for a further 20 minutes, or until the
pineapple is hot, the chicken is tender and the sauce has
thickened. Serve with small portions of cooked rice or noodles,
sprinkled with finely sliced spring onions if you like.

535
CALORIES
PER SERVING

country chicken casserole

SERVES 4

PREP: 20 MINUTES

**HIGH 4–5 HOURS,
PLUS 5 MINUTES
LOW 7–9 HOURS,
PLUS 5 MINUTES**

8 boneless, skinless chicken
    thighs (about 675g)
1 tbsp oil
2 medium onions
600g large waxy potatoes,
    such as Charlotte
4 medium carrots (about
    400g)
2 medium parsnips
3 tbsp plain flour (25g)
1 tsp dried mixed herbs
1 tbsp prepared English
    mustard (from a jar)
100ml hot chicken stock
    (made with 1 chicken
    stock cube)
500ml dry cider
150g frozen peas (thawed)
flaked sea salt
ground black pepper

Tip: To thaw the peas
quickly, put them in a sieve
over the sink and carefully
pour just-boiled water over
them.

A simple, hearty chicken casserole flavoured with cider. It's a
fantastic recipe to put on and then forget about. There's no
need to serve it with extra vegetables, but I often boil some
long-stemmed broccoli or green beans to go alongside.

Trim any excess fat off the chicken thighs with kitchen scissors
and re-form into a neat shape. Season the chicken all over with
a little salt and plenty of pepper. Heat the oil in a large non-stick
frying pan over a medium-high heat and fry the chicken for
about 5 minutes, turning the thighs occasionally until lightly
browned. (Browning smooth side up to start with will help set
the shape.)

While the chicken is frying, prepare the vegetables. Peel and
thinly slice the onions, and peel the potatoes, carrots and
parsnips and cut them into roughly 3cm chunks.

Put all the vegetables except the peas in the slow cooker and
toss with the flour. Add the browned chicken to the pot. Mix the
herbs and mustard with the hot stock, then add the cider and
pour the mixture over the chicken and vegetables.

Cover the pot with a lid and cook on HIGH for 4–5 hours or
LOW for 7–9 hours, or until the chicken is thoroughly cooked
and the vegetables are tender. Remove the lid, stir in the peas,
cover and cook for a further 5 minutes, or until hot.

228
CALORIES
PER SERVING

orange and ginger chicken

SERVES 4

PREP: 10 MINUTES

**HIGH 2-3 HOURS,
PLUS 10 MINUTES**

1 tsp oil
4 boneless, skinless chicken
    breasts (each about 150g)
½ chicken stock cube
150ml just-boiled water
2 tbsp thick-cut orange
    marmalade
1 tbsp dark soy sauce
2 stem ginger balls in syrup
    (from a jar), drained
1 tbsp stem ginger syrup
    (from the jar)
2 tsp cornflour
1 tbsp cold water
flaked sea salt
ground black pepper

This is another store cupboard favourite in my household. Fresh chicken breasts are poached in an orange and ginger-flavoured stock for an easy weekday meal. You can usually find jars of stem ginger in syrup in the jam or baking aisle of the supermarket.

Heat the oil in a large non-stick frying pan. Season the chicken breasts with salt and pepper and fry them over a medium-high heat for 2 minutes on each side, or until lightly browned.

While the chicken is frying put the half stock cube in a heat-proof measuring jug and cover with the just-boiled water. Stir until dissolved then add the marmalade and soy sauce. Cut the stem ginger balls into short strips, then add them to the stock and stir in the syrup.

Transfer the chicken breasts to the slow cooker and pour over the orange and ginger mixture. Cover with the lid and cook on HIGH for 2-3 hours, or until thoroughly cooked and perfectly tender.

Mix the cornflour with the water, remove the slow cooker lid and gently stir the mixture into the slow cooker, taking care not to break up the chicken. Cover again and cook for a further 10 minutes, or until the sauce is thickened and glossy.

Serve with freshly cooked rice and lots of green vegetables.

210

chicken with sticky barbecue sauce

SERVES 4

PREP: 5 MINUTES

HIGH 2-3 HOURS,
PLUS 30 MINUTES

4 boneless, skinless chicken
   breasts (each about 150g)
75g tomato ketchup
2 tbsp Worcestershire sauce
2 tbsp clear honey
1 tsp prepared English
   mustard (from a jar)
¼–½ tsp dried chilli flakes
   (depending on taste)
½ tsp smoked paprika (not
   hot smoked)
flaked sea salt
ground black pepper
2 spring onions or chopped
   parsley, to serve (optional)

Tip: Check the manufacturer's
instructions to make sure
that you can preheat your
slow cooker.

A real family favourite, these tender chicken breasts are smothered in a tangy barbecue-style sauce. They don't take too long to cook – put them on before the school run and they will be ready after the homework has been done. Make the whole batch even if you are cooking for fewer than four, as the cold cooked chicken is great in salads and wraps.

Preheat your slow cooker. Season the chicken breasts with salt and pepper. Place in the slow cooker in a single layer. Cover with the lid and cook on HIGH for 2–3 hours or until thoroughly cooked and perfectly tender.

To make the barbecue sauce, combine the ketchup, Worcestershire sauce, honey, mustard, chilli flakes and paprika. Remove the pot from the slow cooker, carefully drain off any chicken juices and discard them. (You may need to remove the chicken breasts first if you have a heavy pot.)

Replace the pot and pour the barbecue sauce over the chicken, turning a few times until thickly coated. Cover again and cook on HIGH for a further 30 minutes. Sprinkle with sliced spring onions or chopped parsley and serve with a large mixed salad and a few boiled new potatoes.

252

easy chicken with ham and broccoli

3 tsp oil
4 boneless, skinless chicken
   breasts (each about 150g)
2 long (banana) shallots
   or 1 small onion
1 garlic clove
50g sliced smoked ham
½ chicken stock cube
250ml just-boiled water
3 tbsp plain flour (25g)
50ml white wine (or extra
   stock)
250g broccoli
flaked sea salt
ground black pepper

Tip: When the broccoli and chicken are cooked you can add 3 tbsp of half-fat crème fraiche to make this dish extra creamy. Don't forget to add an extra 75 calories per serving.

Chicken and ham always go well together, and this simple recipe makes the perfect midweek supper. The broccoli will lose its colour a little in the slow cooker, but you can always quickly boil it and stir through the hot chicken and ham sauce just before serving if you prefer.

Heat 1 teaspoon of the oil in a large non-stick frying pan. Season the chicken breasts with salt and pepper and fry over a medium-high heat for 2–3 minutes on each side, or until lightly browned.

While the chicken is frying, peel and thinly slice the shallots or onion and peel and crush the garlic. Rip the ham into small pieces. Transfer the chicken breasts to the slow cooker.

Add the remaining oil and the shallots or onion to the frying pan and cook gently for 2 minutes, or until lightly coloured, stirring continuously. Add the garlic and cook for a few seconds more. Add to the chicken.

Dissolve the stock cube in the just-boiled water in a bowl, then use a metal whisk to whisk the flour into the stock until no lumps remain. Stir in the wine. Add the stock to the chicken and stir well. Top with the ham. Cover with the lid and cook on HIGH for 2–3 hours, or until the chicken is thoroughly cooked and perfectly tender.

Cut the broccoli into small florets and stir into the sauce. Cover with the lid and cook for a further 15 minutes or until the broccoli is just tender. Serve with a small portion of new potatoes and more freshly cooked vegetables.

353

coq au vin

SERVES 4

PREP: 20 MINUTES

HIGH 3-4 HOURS
LOW 5-7 HOURS

8 boneless, skinless chicken
   thighs (about 675g)
3 rashers smoked rindless
   back bacon
1 medium onion
2 garlic cloves
16 small shallots (about
   400g)
1 tbsp oil
3 tbsp plain flour (25g)
2 tbsp brandy (optional)
150ml red wine
400g can chopped
   tomatoes
200g baby button
   mushrooms
1 fresh bay leaf or 2 dried
   bay leaves
2-3 bushy thyme sprigs or
   ½ tsp dried thyme
flaked sea salt
ground black pepper

A real classic given the slow cooker treatment. Chicken thighs remain more succulent than breasts after a long cook and are cheaper too. Don't worry if you don't have any brandy handy, just leave it out. Serve with mashed potatoes and green beans, garnished with freshly chopped parsley.

Trim any excess fat off the chicken thighs with kitchen scissors and re-form into a neat shape. Season the chicken all over with a little salt and plenty of pepper. Cut the bacon into short, roughly 2cm-wide strips. Peel and finely chop the onion, peel and crush the garlic and peel the shallots.

Heat the oil in a large non-stick frying pan over a medium-high heat and fry the chicken for about 5 minutes, turning the thighs occasionally until lightly browned. (Browning smooth side up to start with will help set the shape.)

Transfer to the slow cooker. Return the pan to the heat. Add the bacon strips and cook for 2-3 minutes, or until beginning to crisp, turning often. Scatter on top of the chicken.

Next, add the chopped onion to the pan and cook over a medium heat for 4-5 minutes until golden brown, adding the garlic for the last minute of cooking time and stirring often. Tip the onion and garlic into the slow cooker with the chicken pieces, sprinkle the flour over and toss gently together.

Deglaze the frying pan with the brandy, if using, stirring well to remove as much of the tasty sediment from the bottom of the pan as possible. Add half the red wine and bubble for a few seconds more. Pour the hot brandy and wine, and the remaining wine, over the chicken and vegetables.

Stir in the canned tomatoes, shallots, mushrooms, bay leaf and thyme. Cover with the lid and cook on HIGH for 3-4 hours or LOW for 5-7 hours, or until the chicken is thoroughly cooked and the vegetables are tender. Adjust seasoning to taste before serving.

298
CALORIES
PER SERVING

easy slow cooker curry

SERVES 4

PREP: 15 MINUTES

HIGH 3½–4½ HOURS, PLUS 5 MINUTES

2 large onions (each about 200g)

1 tbsp, plus 1 tsp oil

65g (4 tbsp) medium curry paste, such as tikka masala or rogan josh (from a jar)

500g boneless, skinless chicken breasts

350ml just-boiled water

1 tsp caster sugar

½ tsp flaked sea salt, plus extra to season

2 tbsp cornflour

2 tbsp cold water

1–2 tbsp double cream (optional)

ground black pepper

natural yoghurt, to serve

fresh coriander, to garnish (optional)

Flat-freeze the cooked and cooled curry in labelled zip-seal bags for up to 2 months. Thaw overnight in the fridge then reheat in the microwave or a large non-stick saucepan, stirring regularly, until piping hot throughout.

Tip: Use 8 boneless, skinless chicken thighs (well trimmed) if you prefer – they'll be more succulent – but you'll need to add an extra 27 calories to each serving.

A brilliant, flexible curry that uses just a handful of readily available ingredients. Choose whether you want to make it with chicken, lamb or beef – and pick your own strength of curry paste. You will need a food processor to blitz the onions at the beginning, but it's worth the extra washing up.

Peel and cut the onions into large chunks. Put in a food processor and blitz until as finely chopped as possible.

Heat 1 tablespoon of oil in a large non-stick frying pan and fry the onions over a medium-high heat for 6–8 minutes, or until nicely browned, stirring regularly. Add the curry paste and cook for a further 1–2 minutes, stirring continuously. Tip the spiced onions into the slow cooker. Cut the chicken into roughly 3cm chunks.

Return the pan to the heat and add the remaining teaspoon of oil and the chicken pieces. Fry over a high heat for 3–4 minutes, or until the chicken is very lightly coloured all over, turning occasionally.

Add the chicken, water, sugar and salt to the slow cooker. Season with ground black pepper and stir well. Cover and cook on HIGH for 3½–4½ hours, or until the chicken is thoroughly cooked and the spices have mellowed.

Mix the cornflour with the cold water until smooth, and stir into the curry. Add the cream, if using, and adjust the seasoning to taste. Cover and cook for a further 5 minutes or until thickened. Serve with yoghurt, rice and a colourful mixed salad. Garnish with fresh coriander if you like.

Lamb or beef curry: Use 600g trimmed lamb neck fillet or 600g trimmed braising beef, cut into 3cm chunks, and cook on HIGH for 3½–4½ hours or LOW for 5–7 hours for the lamb or 6–8 hours for the beef, until tender. Spoon off any fat that has risen to the surface and thicken the sauce with 1 tablespoon of cornflour mixed with 1 tablespoon of cold water. Serves 4. Calories per serving: 463 (lamb), 367 (beef).

406

CALORIES
PER SERVING

slow chicken pho

SERVES 4
PREP: 20 MINUTES
HIGH 4–5 HOURS,
PLUS 10 MINUTES

2 medium onions
5 garlic cloves
40g chunk of fresh root
  ginger
2 fresh long red chillies
  (deseeded first if you
  like), plus 1–2 extra to
  serve (optional)
½–1 tsp dried chilli flakes
  (depending on taste)
1 tsp Chinese five spice
  powder
1.5 litres cold water
4 tbsp dark soy sauce, plus
  extra to serve
1.25kg small whole chicken
175g dried flat rice noodles
2 tbsp Thai fish sauce
  (nam pla)
250g long-stemmed
  broccoli
100g beansprouts
40g bunch of fresh
  coriander
4 spring onions
1 large lime

Tip: Check the manufacturer's
instructions to make sure that
you can cook a whole
chicken in your slow cooker.

Chicken pho is a Vietnamese dish of chicken and noodles in a richly flavoured stock. It's naturally low in calories and this recipe makes four very generous servings and up to six lighter meals. You can make the stock a day ahead and then reheat and assemble the ingredients when you are ready.

Peel and thickly slice the onions. Peel and thinly slice the garlic and ginger. Slice the red chillies. Place the onions, garlic, ginger and chillies in the slow cooker and add the chilli flakes, five spice powder, water and soy sauce.

Cut the trussing string off the chicken and place it, breast side up, in the slow cooker. Cover with the lid and cook on HIGH for 4–5 hours or until thoroughly cooked and perfectly tender.

Take the chicken gently out of the slow cooker and place on a grooved board or tray. Drain the onions, aromatic herbs and spices and stock carefully through a colander into a large bowl. Strip the skin off the chicken and discard it. Throw away all the cooking vegetables and pass the stock through a fine sieve into a large saucepan. Take the meat off the bones in large pieces, thickly slice and put it to one side.

Soften or cook the noodles in hot water as directed on the packet, stirring frequently to separate the strands. Skim off the fat from the stock with a large metal spoon and stir in the fish sauce. Bring to a gentle simmer. Trim the long-stemmed broccoli and add to the pan. Cook for 3–5 minutes, or until just tender. Add the chicken to the hot stock and heat thoroughly. Reduce the heat to very low.

Drain the noodles in a sieve and divide between 4 large warmed bowls.

Using tongs, place the broccoli, chicken, beansprouts and coriander leaves in the bowls. Ladle the hot stock over the top and sprinkle with sliced spring onions and sliced fresh chillies (if using). Serve with extra soy sauce and lime, cut into wedges for squeezing.

347
CALORIES
PER SERVING

barley chicken and mushroom risotto

SERVES: 4

PREP: 25 MINUTES

HIGH 2½ – 3½ HOURS, PLUS 5 MINUTES

10g dried porcini
    mushrooms
250ml just-boiled water
6 boneless, skinless chicken
    thighs (about 500g)
1 medium onion
250g closed cup or small
    Portobello mushrooms
1 tbsp oil
2 garlic cloves
150g pearl barley
50ml Marsala, Madeira,
    white wine or extra
    chicken stock
500ml hot chicken stock
    (made with 1 chicken
    stock cube)
2 medium leeks (optional)
150ml cold water (optional)
flaked sea salt
ground black pepper

Pearl barley works better than rice for this long-cooking risotto, and adds a silkiness to the sauce. The dried mushrooms can be found in larger supermarkets and give the dish a rich, luxurious taste. Serve it with a large mixed salad.

Put the dried mushrooms in a heat-proof measuring jug and add the just-boiled water. Leave to stand for roughly 20 minutes while you prepare the other ingredients. Trim any excess fat off the chicken thighs with kitchen scissors and cut each thigh into four evenly-sized pieces. Season all over with salt and pepper.

Peel and finely chop the onion and thickly slice the mushrooms. Heat the oil in a large non-stick frying pan and fry the onion and mushrooms for 5 minutes, or until softened and lightly browned. Peel and crush the garlic, add to the pan and cook for a few seconds more, stirring. Tip into the slow cooker. Add the chicken pieces.

Strain the rehydrated mushrooms through a sieve, reserving the soaking water, and roughly chop them. Add the chopped mushrooms and their liquor to the slow cooker and stir in the pearl barley, Marsala, Madeira or wine (if using) and chicken stock.

Cover with the lid and cook on HIGH for 2½–3½ hours, or until the chicken is thoroughly cooked, the barley is tender and the stock has thickened. Just before the risotto is ready, trim and finely slice the leeks, if using. Pour the water into a frying pan and cook the leeks for 4–5 minutes, or until tender, stirring occasionally. Drain well. Serve the risotto in warmed bowls, topped with the leeks.

lamb

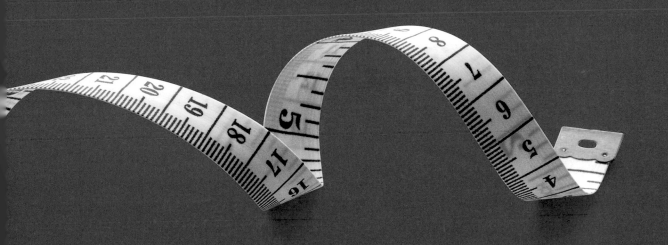

504

no hurry lamb curry

2 medium onions
2 garlic cloves
25g chunk of fresh root
    ginger
25g bunch of fresh
    coriander
1 tbsp oil
800g lamb neck fillet
3 tbsp medium Indian curry
    paste (from a jar)
400g can chopped
    tomatoes
1 tsp caster sugar
150g dried red split lentils
250ml hot lamb stock
    (made with 1 lamb stock
    cube)
flaked sea salt
ground black pepper

Freeze the cooled curry in
a labelled zip-seal bag or
in freezer-proof containers
for up to 3 months. Thaw in
the fridge overnight.
Reheat thoroughly in the
microwave or a large
saucepan with an extra
150ml just-boiled water,
stirring occasionally, until
piping hot.

This is a rich-tasting curry with tender lamb and lentils. I've
used lamb neck fillet as it stays tender during the long cooking
time, but you could use leg meat instead. For a more saucy
curry, add an extra 100ml of stock. Serve with small portions of
freshly cooked basmati rice, topped with yoghurt, cucumber
and mint. Freeze any leftovers for another day.

Peel and thinly slice the onions, peel and crush the garlic, peel
and finely grate the ginger, and roughly chop the coriander
(including the stalks). Pour the oil into a large non-stick frying
pan and fry the onions over a medium-high heat for 5 minutes,
or until softened and lightly browned, stirring frequently.

While the onions are cooking, trim the lamb neck of any hard
fat that you can get to easily and cut the meat into roughly 3cm
chunks. Season with salt and plenty of pepper. Put into the slow
cooker.

Add the garlic, ginger and curry paste to the onions and cook
for a further minute, stirring continuously. Add to the slow
cooker and stir in the canned tomatoes, caster sugar and
chopped coriander. Rinse the lentils in a sieve under cold
running water and add them to the pot.

Pour over the stock, stir well and cover with the lid. Cook on
HIGH for 4–5 hours or LOW for 8–10 hours, or until the lamb and
lentils are very tender. If you get a chance, stir the curry halfway
through the cooking time, quickly replacing the lid. Season with
more salt and pepper to taste just before serving.

235

slow-cooked lamb with pomegranate

1kg half leg of lamb
2 rosemary sprigs
1 garlic bulb
2-3 bushy thyme sprigs
50ml white wine or water
flaked sea salt
ground black pepper
100g pomegranate seeds,
    to serve (optional)
fresh mint leaves, yoghurt
    flatbreads (see page 101)
    or warmed pitta bread, to
    serve
1 tbsp pomegranate
    molasses (optional)

Tip: You can squeeze the softened garlic out of its skin to serve with the lamb, if you like.

Check the manufacturer's instructions to make sure that you can preheat your slow cooker.

If you know you will be out all day, this is a fab recipe to put on first thing. It will sit happily for hours, ready for you to shred and pile on to warmed pitta bread with hummus and yoghurt. Pomegranate seeds and pomegranate molasses are a nice addition but not totally necessary, so leave them out if it's easier. Any leftover cold lamb can be used for salads or sandwiches the next day and it reheats well, too.

Preheat your slow cooker on HIGH. Place the lamb in the slow cooker, strip the rosemary needles off the stalks and sprinkle them over the top. Separate the cloves of the garlic bulb and add them along with the thyme sprigs. Pour over the wine or water, season well with salt and pepper and cook on HIGH for 4-5 hours or LOW for 8-10 hours, or until very tender.

Remove the slow cooker lid, transfer the lamb to a warmed serving dish and shred the meat with two forks, discarding the thin skin, bone and thyme stalks. Strain over the cooking liquor from the slow cooker pot, and sprinkle with pomegranate seeds (if using) and fresh mint leaves.

Serve on warm yoghurt flatbread or warmed pitta bread, spread with hummus and topped with yoghurt and a dribble of pomegranate molasses (if using).

238

minted lamb koftas

SERVES 4

PREP: 20 MINUTES

HIGH 3–4 HOURS
LOW 6–8 HOURS

1 medium onion
2 garlic cloves
450g minced lamb
  (about 20% fat)
1 lemon
1 tsp ground cumin
1 tsp ground coriander
½ tsp hot chilli powder
¼ tsp ground cinnamon
20g bunch of fresh mint,
  plus extra to garnish
flaked sea salt
ground black pepper
fresh lemon wedges and
  mixed salad, to serve

Open-freeze the raw
lamb koftas on a baking
parchment-lined tray until
solid, then pack into a
labelled freezer bag and
freeze for up to 1 month.
Thaw overnight in the fridge
and cook as above.

Lamb koftas make a great alternative to burgers. They're
delicious served hot and almost as nice cold. The long, slow
cooking makes them extra tender and brings out all the
flavours. Freeze half for cooking another day if you like.

Peel and finely chop the onion and peel and crush the garlic.
Put the onion and garlic in a large bowl with the lamb mince.
Finely grate the lemon zest and sprinkle over. Add the cumin,
coriander, chilli powder and cinnamon to the lamb mixture.

Strip the mint leaves off the stalks and finely chop them. You
should end up with about 3 heaped tablespoons of mint leaves.
Add them to the bowl with the mince.

Season with a good pinch of flaked sea salt and plenty of
pepper and mix until well combined. Form the meat mixture
into 20 balls, or shape into ovals if you prefer.

Transfer the koftas to the slow cooker, placing them on top of
each other if necessary. Cover with the lid and cook on HIGH for
3–4 hours or LOW for 6–8 hours, or until thoroughly cooked
and very tender. Serve hot or cold with a large mixed salad,
minted cucumber and yoghurt sauce (see below), lemon
wedges for squeezing and the reserved mint to garnish.

Minted cucumber and yoghurt sauce: Cut a third of a large
cucumber into small chunks and put the chunks in a bowl. Add
2 heaped tablespoons of chopped fresh mint and 150g low-fat
plain bio yoghurt and mix well. Serves 4. Calories per serving: 25

518
CALORIES
PER SERVING

garrie's lamb hot pot

SERVES 4
PREP: 20 MINUTES
HIGH 3-4 HOURS,
PLUS 5 MINUTES
LOW 6-8 HOURS,
PLUS 5 MINUTES

600g lamb neck fillet
2 tsp oil
2 medium onions
4 medium carrots
  (about 400g)
3 medium potatoes
  (about 500g)
3 tbsp plain flour (25g)
300ml hot lamb stock
  (made with 1 lamb
  stock cube)
1 tbsp fresh thyme leaves or
  ½ tsp dried thyme
1 tsp dried mint
2 tbsp Worcestershire sauce
100g frozen peas (thawed)
flaked sea salt
ground black pepper

Tip: You don't have to
brown the lamb in a frying
pan first, but I think it adds
an extra layer of flavour to
this dish.

This lamb hot pot is based on my grandmother's recipe.
She used to make her version in a pressure cooker, but it works
brilliantly well in a slow cooker. The lamb becomes deliciously
tender and the minted vegetables complement it perfectly.
It's one of my all-time favourite recipes, and one I return to
time after time.

Trim the lamb of any hard fat and sinew that you can easily
reach, and cut into roughly 3cm chunks. Season the meat
generously all over with salt and pepper.

Heat the oil in a large non-stick frying pan and fry the lamb over
a medium-high heat for 6–8 minutes, or until nicely browned on
all sides. Transfer to the slow cooker.

Peel and thinly slice the onions, peel and cut the carrots into
roughly 1cm-thick diagonal slices, and peel and cut the
potatoes into roughly 3cm chunks.

Tip the onions, carrots and potatoes into the slow cooker with
the lamb, and sprinkle with the flour. Toss together well. Pour
over the stock and add the thyme, mint, Worcestershire sauce
and a few twists of pepper, and stir together well.

Cover with the lid and cook on HIGH for 3–4 hours or LOW for
6–8 hours, or until the lamb and vegetables are very tender.
You will probably find the vegetables take longer than the
lamb. Remove the slow cooker lid, add the peas, cover again
and cook for a further 5 minutes.

429

lamb tagine with sweet potatoes

SERVES 6
PREP: 15 MINUTES
HIGH 3½-4½ HOURS
LOW 6-8 HOURS

800g lamb neck fillet
2 medium onions
4 garlic cloves
300g sweet potatoes
400g can chickpeas
25g bunch of fresh
   coriander, plus extra to
   garnish
4 tsp ras-el-hanout spice
   mix
1 tsp cumin seeds
100ml hot lamb stock
   (made with 1 lamb stock
   cube)
2 x 400g cans chopped
   tomatoes
4 tsp harissa paste (from
   a jar)
2 tbsp clear honey
flaked sea salt
ground black pepper

Freeze the cooked and cooled tagine in large, labelled zip-seal bags or freezer-proof containers for up to 2 months. Thaw overnight in the fridge then reheat in the microwave or a large saucepan with an extra 150ml water, stirring occasionally, until piping hot.

This recipe is based on one of my favourite lamb tagine recipes. It uses ras-el-hanout spice mix and harissa paste, which are available in larger supermarkets. Both will last for ages in the store cupboard or fridge. Serve with a large mixed salad and small portions of couscous or rice. I often accompany mine with spoonfuls of natural yoghurt, too. Freeze any leftovers for another day.

Trim the lamb neck fillet of any hard fat or sinew that you can easily reach, and cut the lamb into roughly 4cm chunks. Peel and thinly slice the onions and peel and crush the garlic. Peel and cut the sweet potato into roughly 3cm chunks. Rinse the chickpeas in a sieve under cold running water, and drain. Finely chop the coriander, including the stalks.

Place the lamb, vegetables, chickpeas and all the other ingredients in the slow cooker. Season with a good pinch of salt and plenty of pepper and mix until well combined.

Cover with the lid and cook on HIGH for 3½-4½ hours or LOW for 6-8 hours, or until the lamb and vegetables are very tender and the sauce is thick and aromatic. Scatter with fresh coriander just before serving.

337

lamb provençal

525g lamb leg steaks
3 tbsp plain flour (25g)
1 large onion
2 garlic cloves
1 lamb stock cube
150ml just-boiled water
1 tbsp Marmite
2 tbsp tomato purée
400g can butterbeans
400g can chopped
    tomatoes
2 tsp dried mixed herbs
150ml red wine, or extra
    lamb stock
1 large red and 1 large yellow
    pepper
2 medium courgettes
flaked sea salt
ground black pepper

Freeze the cooked and
cooled casserole in labelled
zip-seal bags or freezer-
proof containers for up to
3 months. Thaw overnight
in the fridge and reheat in
the microwave, stirring
occasionally, until piping hot.

**This simple one-pot dish is made from slowly simmered lamb
in a rich tomato sauce with peppers, courgettes, red wine
and herbs.**

Trim any hard fat off the lamb, then cut the lamb into roughly
3cm chunks and put it in the slow cooker. Add the flour and
plenty of salt and pepper and toss to coat the pieces. Peel and
very thinly slice the onion and peel and crush the garlic.

Dissolve the stock cube in the just-boiled water and stir in the
Marmite and tomato purée. Rinse the butterbeans in a sieve
under running water, then drain. Add the beans, onion, garlic,
stock mixture, tomatoes, herbs and wine (or extra stock) to the
slow cooker and stir to combine.

Halve and deseed the peppers then cut them into roughly 4cm
chunks. Trim and thickly slice the courgettes. Place the peppers
and courgettes on top of the lamb but do not stir. Cover with
the lid and cook on HIGH for 4–5 hours or LOW for 5–7 hours,
or until the lamb is very tender and the onions are softened.

Adjust the seasoning to taste and serve with small portions of
cooked rice, mash or boiled potatoes.

minted slow-roast lamb

SERVES: 6

PREP: 20 MINUTES

**HIGH 3-4 HOURS,
PLUS 10 MINUTES
LOW 6-7 HOURS,
PLUS 10 MINUTES**

2 tsp oil
1kg boneless, rolled and tied
  leg of lamb
1 medium onion
2 garlic cloves
100ml red wine
25g bunch of fresh mint
100ml lamb stock (made
  with ½ lamb stock cube)
1 tbsp redcurrant jelly
4 tsp cornflour
1½ tbsp cold water
flaked sea salt
ground black pepper

FOR THE MINT SAUCE
25g bunch of fresh mint
2 tsp caster sugar
1 tbsp white wine vinegar
5 tbsp just-boiled water

Tip: If your lamb doesn't fit
in the slow cooker in one
piece, cut it in half and cook
the two pieces side by
side instead.

Boned and rolled lamb leg
isn't cheap, but there isn't
any waste, so it's a lovely
dish to save for a special
occasion. Or buy it when it
is on offer and freeze it to
cook later.

**This is a brilliantly simple way to make a Sunday roast.
The lamb is really succulent and is easy to carve.**

Heat the oil in a large non-stick frying pan. Season the lamb on
all sides with salt and pepper. Brown the lamb in the pan over a
medium heat for 8–10 minutes, turning it every couple of
minutes until golden.

Peel and thinly slice the onion and garlic and place in the slow
cooker, then place the lamb on top, tucking the onion under the
lamb. Deglaze the frying pan with the wine, bubbling for a few
seconds and stirring continuously. Pour the wine around the lamb.

Strip the mint leaves and roughly chop them, then sprinkle over
the lamb. Cover with the lid and cook on HIGH for 3–4 hours or
LOW for 6–7 hours, or until the lamb is cooked through and
very tender.

Remove the slow cooker lid, take the lamb out and put it on a
board or warmed platter. Flick off the mint leaves, which will
have turned dark. Cover the lamb with foil and a couple of tea
towels to keep warm. Carefully strain the cooking liquor from
the slow cooker through a fine sieve into a small saucepan.
Leave to stand for 5–10 minutes.

While the liquor is standing, make the mint sauce. Strip the mint
leaves and roughly chop them. Mix with the sugar and vinegar
in a small bowl and stir in the just-boiled water. Set aside.

To make the gravy, tilt the pan with the lamb liquor and
carefully spoon off and discard any fat that has risen to the
surface. Add the stock and the redcurrant jelly to the pan, bring
to a simmer and cook for 3 minutes.

Mix the cornflour with the water until smooth and add to the
pan. Cook for a further 1–2 minutes, stirring until thickened.
Season and strain into a warmed heat-proof jug.

Uncover the lamb and spoon the mint sauce over the top.
Serve carved in slices, with lots of fresh vegetables and the
gravy for pouring.

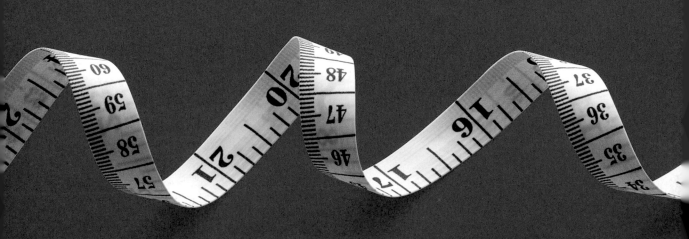

beef

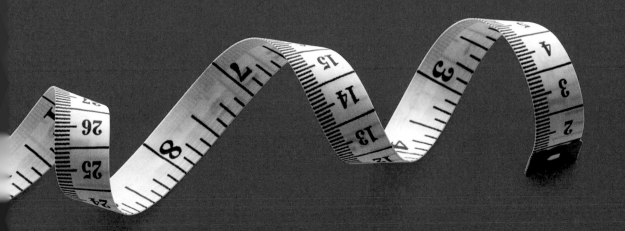

367
CALORIES
PER SERVING

slow teriyaki beef

SERVES 4
PREP: 10 MINUTES
HIGH 5-6 HOURS,
PLUS 10 MINUTES
LOW 7-9 HOURS,
PLUS 10 MINUTES

25g chunk of fresh root
  ginger
3 garlic cloves
4 tbsp dark soy sauce
  (or wheat-free tamari)
250ml cold water
50g sultanas
½ tsp dried chilli flakes
2 medium red onions
1 tsp Chinese five spice
  powder
4 x 175g thick slices good-
  quality braising steak
2 tbsp cornflour
2 tbsp cold water
ground black pepper
2-3 spring onions, to serve

Freeze the cooked and
cooled beef in labelled zip-
seal bags or freezer-proof
containers for up to 3
months. Thaw overnight in
the fridge then reheat in the
microwave or a frying pan
over a medium heat, stirring
occasionally, until piping
hot. Don't worry if the meat
breaks up a little.

Tip: Using sultanas to
sweeten the sauce cuts out
any refined sugar, but you
can add 2 tablespoons of
soft, light brown sugar
instead if you like, and
skip the blitzing stage.

A luscious Asian-inspired dish with a rich savoury flavour, this teriyaki beef is ideal for a long slow cook when you have a busy day. Serve simply with boiled noodles or rice and some freshly cooked greens.

Peel and finely grate the root ginger and garlic and put in a small saucepan with the soy sauce, water, sultanas and chilli flakes. Bring to the boil and cook for 3 minutes to soften the sultanas.

Remove from the heat and blitz with a stick blender until as smooth as possible. (Alternatively, cool for a few minutes and blitz in a food processor.) Pour the soy mixture into the slow cooker. Peel and cut the onions into thin wedges. Add the onions and five spice powder to the slow cooker.

Trim any hard fat off the beef and season the meat well with pepper. Add to the slow cooker and turn a couple of times. Keep the beef in large pieces so it cooks slowly. Cover with the lid and cook on HIGH for 5-6 hours or LOW for 7-9 hours, or until the beef is very tender.

Mix the cornflour with the water, remove the slow cooker lid and gently stir it into the sauce, taking care not to break up the beef too much. Cover again and cook for a further 10 minutes, or until the sauce is thickened and glossy.

Transfer the beef and sauce to a warmed serving platter. Sprinkle with sliced spring onions and serve with small portions of rice or noodles.

403
CALORIES
PER SERVING

bolognese pasta pot

SERVES 5
PREP: 10 MINUTES
**HIGH 4–5 HOURS,
PLUS 30 MINUTES
LOW 6–8 HOURS,
PLUS 30 MINUTES ON HIGH**

450g lean minced beef
    (10% fat or less)
1 large onion
150g closed cup
    mushrooms
2 garlic cloves
150ml red wine or extra beef
    stock
500ml hot beef stock
    (made with 1 beef stock
    cube)
400g can chopped
    tomatoes
3 tbsp tomato purée
1½ tsp dried oregano
1 tbsp cornflour
1 tbsp cold water
250g dried penne pasta
flaked sea salt
ground black pepper
large mixed salad, to serve

Tip: This is delicious served topped with a dribble of fresh pesto sauce. You can find tubs in the chiller cabinets of larger supermarkets or make your own.

Add dried pasta to your Bolognese sauce, cook them together for an extra 20–30 minutes, and you'll have a delicious and easy supper with very little washing up. Try using whole wheat penne for this recipe, for extra fibre.

Put the mince in a frying pan over a medium heat and fry for 3–5 minutes, stirring and squishing it against the side of the pan with two wooden spoons to break up the beef. Peel and finely chop the onion, thickly slice the mushrooms and peel and crush the garlic. Transfer the mince to the slow cooker and add the onions, mushrooms and garlic.

Add the wine (if using) and the beef stock. Tip in the tomatoes and stir in the tomato purée, oregano and lots of ground black pepper. Cover with the lid and cook on HIGH for 4–5 hours or LOW for 6–8 hours, or until the mince and onions are very tender.

Mix the cornflour and water until smooth, then remove the slow cooker lid and stir the mixture into the Bolognese. Add the pasta and stir well. Cover again and continue to cook on HIGH for 20–30 minutes, or until the pasta is softened, stirring after 15 minutes. Adjust the seasoning to taste and serve with a large mixed salad.

362

italian beef with orange

SERVES 6

PREP: 20 MINUTES

HIGH 4-5 HOURS
LOW 8-10 HOURS

1.2kg good-quality braising
    steak (such as chuck
    steak)
2 medium onions
2 celery sticks
1 medium orange
1 tsp coriander seeds
1 tsp flaked sea salt, plus
    extra to season
2 tsp dried mixed herbs
½ tsp dried chilli flakes
1 bay leaf
200ml red wine
2 x 400g cans chopped
    tomatoes
3 tbsp plain flour (25g)
100ml hot beef stock (made
    with 1 beef stock cube)
ground black pepper
chopped fresh parsley,
    to garnish

Flat-freeze the cooked and
cooled casserole in labelled
zip-seal bags for up to 3
months. Thaw overnight in
the fridge and then reheat
in the microwave or a large
saucepan over a medium
heat, stirring occasionally,
until piping hot throughout.

Tip: If the sauce is a little
thin at the end of cooking,
stir in 1-2 tbsp cornflour
mixed with 1-2 tbsp cold
water, cover and cook for
a further 10 minutes.

This is a wonderfully rich Italian-style beef stew flavoured with
orange zest. The long cooking tenderises the meat and gives
the tomatoes sweetness. Buy good braising beef if you can
– the kind you need to cut yourself, rather than ready-diced
beef; the larger chunks will cook more slowly, allowing the
sauce to become rich and sweet. Serve with small portions
of pasta, potatoes or rice, and a mixed green salad.

Trim any hard fat from the beef and cut the meat into roughly
4cm chunks. Season well with salt and black pepper. Place in
the slow cooker.

Peel and thinly slice the onions and trim and thinly slice the
celery. Peel two long strips off the orange with a potato peeler.
Cut the orange in half and squeeze the juice. Lightly crush the
coriander seeds with a pestle and mortar.

Add the onions, celery, orange zest and juice to the beef along
with all the remaining ingredients, except the parsley. Season
with lots of ground black pepper and mix until well combined.

Cover with the lid and cook on HIGH for 4-5 hours or LOW for
8-10 hours, or until the beef is beautifully tender and the sauce
has thickened. Adjust the seasoning to taste and garnish with
roughly chopped parsley if you like.

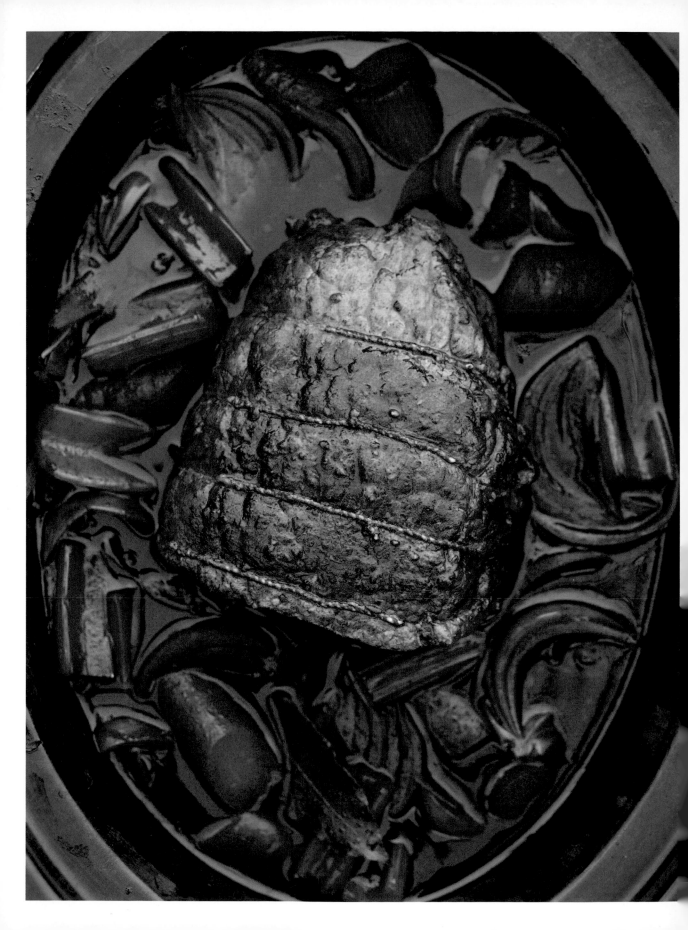

360
CALORIES
PER SERVING

beef pot roast

SERVES 6
PREP: 15 MINUTES
LOW 8–10 HOURS

1.2kg lean boneless beef
   silverside, rolled and tied
1 tsp flaked sea salt,
   plus extra to season
2 tsp oil
3 medium onions
5 medium carrots (about
   500g)
6 celery sticks
3 fresh bushy thyme sprigs
   or 1 tsp dried thyme
1 large bay leaf
2 tbsp tomato purée
175ml red wine (or extra
   beef stock)
150ml hot beef stock (made
   with 1 beef stock cube)
ground black pepper
flat-leaf parsley, to garnish
   (optional)

Tip: Use 500g of whole
stubby Chantenay carrots
instead of the sliced carrots,
if you like.

This is an easy way to cut the calories in your usual Sunday roast, and it is one of those dishes you can bung on and forget all day. Made with great-value silverside, it's a cheaper way to feed a crowd than using a prime joint. Any leftover cold beef can be reheated or used for sandwiches and salads the next day. Serve with freshly cooked green beans or shredded Savoy cabbage, and small portions of mashed or boiled potatoes.

Season the beef all over with the salt and plenty of pepper. Heat the oil in a large non-stick frying pan and brown the beef for 6–8 minutes, turning occasionally until it is well coloured all over. While the beef is browning, peel the onions and cut each one into roughly 12 wedges from root to tip, peel and cut the carrots into roughly 4cm lengths, and trim and cut the celery into roughly 4cm lengths.

Transfer the beef to the slow cooker and add the onions, carrots, celery, thyme and bay leaf, placing them around the joint. Stir the tomato purée and wine (if using) into the hot beef stock and pour around the beef. Cover with the lid and cook on LOW for 8–10 hours, or until the beef is very tender and yields easily to the pressure of a fork.

Remove the lid, lift the beef out of the dish with a couple of forks and place it on a board or serving platter. If you prefer a thicker gravy, transfer the cooked vegetables to a warmed serving dish with a slotted spoon, cover and keep warm. Carefully pour the cooking liquor into a large saucepan. Bring to the boil and cook for 4–5 minutes, or until it reaches your preferred consistency.

Cut the string around the beef and carve the meat into slices. Serve with the poached vegetables and the rich cooking liquor for gravy. Garnish with freshly chopped parsley, if you like.

468

beef bourguignon

SERVES 6
PREP: 20-25 MINUTES
HIGH 4-5 HOURS,
PLUS 10 MINUTES
LOW 5-7 HOURS,
PLUS 10 MINUTES

1.2kg good-quality braising
    steak (such as chuck
    steak)
2 tbsp oil
2 large onions
75g rindless smoked back
    bacon rashers
400g button mushrooms
4 garlic cloves
1 large fresh bay leaf or
    2 dried bay leaves
3 bushy thyme sprigs or
    2 tsp dried thyme
3 tbsp tomato purée
100ml hot beef stock (made
    with 1 beef stock cube)
250ml red wine
3 tbsp cornflour
3 tbsp cold water
flaked sea salt
ground black pepper
fresh flat-leaf parsley,
    to serve (optional)

Freeze the cooked and
cooled bourguignon in
labelled zip-seal bags or
freezer-proof containers for
up to 4 months. Thaw
overnight in the fridge then
reheat in the microwave or a
large saucepan over a
medium heat, stirring, until
piping hot.

**This is definitely a dish that conjures up memories of my
childhood, as it was my mother's go-to recipe for nearly every
party. And why not? It's special enough to spoil your guests
and easy enough to take the pressure off you. Cooking it in a
slow cooker makes the whole process even more hassle-free.
Celeriac purée makes a lovely and lower-calorie alternative to
mashed potatoes.**

Cut the meat into roughly 4-5cm chunks, trimming off any
hard fat or sinew as you go. Season with salt and pepper. Heat
1 tablespoon of the oil into a large non-stick frying pan and fry
the beef over a high heat in two batches for 2-3 minutes, or
until browned on all sides. Transfer to the slow cooker.

While the beef is browning, peel and thinly slice the onions, cut
the bacon rashers into short, roughly 2cm wide strips, halve or
quarter the mushrooms if large, and peel and crush the garlic.

Add 2 teaspoons of the remaining oil and the onions to the
frying pan and cook for 4-5 minutes, or until softened, stirring
frequently. Tip into the slow cooker. Add the remaining oil and
the mushrooms and bacon to the pan and cook for 4-5 minutes
more, or until lightly browned, stirring occasionally. Add the
garlic, bay leaf and thyme and cook for a few seconds more.
Stir into the beef and onions.

Stir the tomato purée into the hot stock and add the wine. Pour
over the beef and stir well. Cover with the lid and cook on HIGH
for 4-5 hours or LOW for 5-7 hours, or until the beef is very
tender.

Mix the cornflour with the water until smooth, remove the slow
cooker lid and stir into the beef. Cover again and cook for a
further 10-15 minutes, or until the sauce has thickened. Adjust
the seasoning to taste and serve with creamy mashed potatoes
or celeriac mash, scattered with freshly chopped parsley (if
using).

495
CALORIES
PER SERVING

beef and mushroom puff pie

SERVES 5

PREP: 30 MINUTES

**HIGH 4-5 HOURS,
PLUS 15 MINUTES
LOW 7-9 HOURS,
PLUS 15 MINUTES**

2 medium onions
2 garlic cloves
1 tbsp oil
700g good-quality beef
    braising steak (such
    as chuck steak)
300g small mushrooms,
    halved or quartered if
    large
3 tbsp plain flour (25g)
2 tsp mixed dried herbs
150ml just-boiled water
1 beef stock cube
1 tbsp Marmite
2 tbsp tomato purée
75ml red wine or extra stock
ground black pepper

FOR THE PASTRY
320g sheet ready-rolled
    puff pastry
oil, for greasing
beaten egg, to glaze

This pie almost didn't make it into the book because I thought it would be impossible to make a pie in a slow cooker. I've cheated with the method slightly and cooked the pastry separately from the beef filling.

Peel and thinly slice the onions, and peel and crush the garlic. Heat the oil in a large non-stick frying pan and fry the onions over a medium heat for 5 minutes, stirring frequently. Add the garlic and cook for a few seconds more. Transfer to the slow cooker.

Trim any hard fat from the beef and cut the meat into roughly 3cm chunks. Season with pepper. Transfer the beef to the slow cooker with the onions and add the mushrooms, the flour and the mixed dried herbs. Toss well together.

Pour the just-boiled water into a small heat-proof measuring jug, add the stock cube, Marmite and tomato purée, and stir until dissolved. Add the red wine (if using) or extra stock, then pour the liquid over the beef and stir well. Cover with the lid and cook on HIGH for 4-5 hours or LOW for 7-9 hours, or until the meat is very tender and the sauce has thickened. (If cooking on LOW, cover the meat with a piece of baking parchment before placing the lid on top. This will help keep it moist.)

Once the beef filling is ready, leave the slow cooker on LOW or switch to WARM. Preheat the oven to 220°C/Fan 200°C/Gas 7 and unroll the puff pastry. Place an upturned 1.2-litre pie dish on top and cut around it with a sharp knife, leaving a 1cm border to allow for shrinkage when baked. Place the pastry on a lightly oiled baking tray. Score the surface lightly with a crisscross pattern and knock up the edges with a horizontally-held knife. Brush with beaten egg and bake for 15-20 minutes, or until well risen and golden brown.

Spoon the cooked beef and mushroom mixture into a warmed 1.2-litre pie dish. Top with the puff pastry lid and serve with lots of freshly cooked vegetables.

331

hungarian beef goulash

SERVES 6
PREP: 15 MINUTES
HIGH 4–5 HOURS
LOW 7–9 HOURS

100ml just-boiled water
1 beef stock cube
1 tbsp Marmite
2 tbsp tomato purée
900g good-quality
    braising steak (ideally
    chuck steak)
2 medium onions
3 tbsp plain flour (25g)
2 tsp hot smoked paprika
1 tbsp paprika (not smoked)
400g can chopped
    tomatoes
2 red and 2 yellow peppers
flaked sea salt
ground black pepper
fresh flat-leaf parsley, to
    garnish (optional)

Flat-freeze the cooked and cooled goulash in labelled zip-seal bags for up to 3 months. Thaw overnight in the fridge then reheat in the microwave or a large saucepan over a medium heat, stirring, until piping hot. Alternatively, warm through from frozen with an extra 200ml water over a medium-low heat until thawed. Then simmer until piping hot throughout, stirring regularly.

This is the perfect dish to make ahead and reheat from frozen. Flat-frozen in zip-seal bags, it can be reheated straight from the freezer and ready in under 20 minutes. Serve with extra vegetables or a small portion of rice and spoonfuls of soured cream (but don't forget to add the extra calories).

Pour the just-boiled water into a small heat-proof measuring jug, add the stock cube, Marmite and tomato purée and stir until dissolved, then set aside.

Trim any hard fat from the beef and cut the meat into roughly 3cm chunks. Season well with salt and pepper and put in the slow cooker. Peel and finely chop the onions and add to the beef. Add the flour and both paprikas and toss together well. Stir in the tomatoes and stock mixture.

Deseed the peppers and cut into roughly 3cm chunks. Scatter on top of the meat and vegetables but do not mix. Cover with the lid and cook on HIGH for 4–5 hours or LOW for 7–9 hours, or until the beef is very tender and the sauce has thickened. Stir and adjust the seasoning to taste. Garnish with freshly chopped parsley, if you like.

341
CALORIES
PER SERVING

beef and ale stew

SERVES 6

PREP: 15 MINUTES

HIGH 4–5 HOURS

LOW 8–10 HOURS

100ml just-boiled water
1 beef stock cube
1 tbsp Marmite
900g good-quality braising beef (such as chuck steak)
4 medium carrots (about 400g)
4 celery sticks
2 medium onions
4 tbsp plain flour (35g)
1 tsp flaked sea salt, plus extra to season
2 tbsp fresh thyme leaves or 1 tsp dried thyme
1 bay leaf
500ml bottle of stout or dark ale, such as Guinness
2 tsp caster sugar
ground black pepper

Freeze the cooked and cooled stew in labelled zip-seal bags or freezer-proof containers for up to 3 months. Thaw overnight in the fridge then reheat in the microwave or a wide-based saucepan over a medium heat, stirring occasionally until piping hot.

This is a lovely traditional stew made with good old-fashioned stout. It's a classic British recipe that works brilliantly in a slow cooker. Use good-quality braising steak and not extra-lean steak, as a little bit of fat will keep the meat moist as it cooks and add flavour to the stew. Serve with smooth mashed potatoes to mop up all the lovely sauce.

Pour the just-boiled water into a heat-proof measuring jug, add the stock cube and Marmite, stir until dissolved and set aside. Trim any hard fat from the beef and cut the meat into roughly 3cm chunks. Peel and cut the carrots into roughly 3cm lengths, trim and cut the celery into 3cm lengths, and peel and thinly slice the onions.

Add the beef and vegetables to the slow cooker and toss with the flour, salt, thyme and plenty of pepper. Add the bay leaf, stout or ale, stock mixture and sugar. Stir well.

Cover with the lid and cook on HIGH for 4–5 hours or LOW for 8–10 hours, until the beef is very tender and the vegetables are cooked. Serve with potatoes and lots of seasonal vegetables.

405

chunky beef chilli

2 medium onions
2 garlic cloves
1kg good-quality braising
  steak (ideally chuck
  steak)
3 tbsp plain flour (25g)
2 tsp ground cumin
2 tsp ground coriander
2 tsp hot chilli powder
2 tsp smoked paprika (not
  hot smoked)
100ml red wine or extra
  beef stock
100ml hot beef stock (made
  with 1 beef stock cube)
400g can chopped
  tomatoes
2 tsp caster sugar
1 tsp dried oregano
2 x 400g cans red kidney
  beans
2 tbsp fresh lime juice
flaked sea salt
ground black pepper

Freeze the cooked and
cooled chilli in labelled zip-
seal bags or freezer-proof
containers for up to
3 months. Defrost in the
fridge overnight and reheat
in the microwave or a large
saucepan over a medium
heat, stirring occasionally,
until piping hot.

My chilli is a little different because I use chunks of beef instead of mince. If you have never made it this way, give it a go – I think it makes the dish far more satisfying, and it freezes brilliantly too.

Peel and finely chop the onions, and peel and finely chop the garlic. Trim the beef of any hard fat and cut the meat into roughly 4cm chunks. Place in the slow cooker and toss with the flour and spices, a good pinch of salt and plenty of pepper.

Add the red wine (if using) and stock to the slow cooker along with the chopped tomatoes, sugar and oregano. Drain and rinse the kidney beans in a sieve under cold running water, and add them too. Season with salt and plenty of pepper.

Cover with the lid and cook on HIGH for 5–6 hours or LOW for 8–10 hours. Remove the lid and check that the beef is very tender and that the sauce has thickened. Stir in the lime juice and adjust the seasoning to taste.

Serve the chilli with small portions of rice and a fresh tomato and sliced onion salsa. Serve bowls of sliced avocado and soured cream or natural yoghurt alongside, but don't forget to add the extra calories. Sprinkle with thinly sliced chillies if you like it extra fiery.

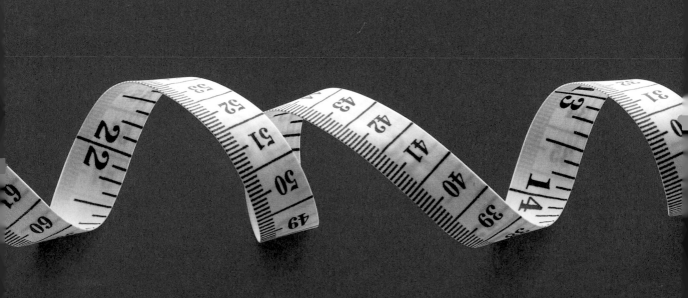

pork
and ham

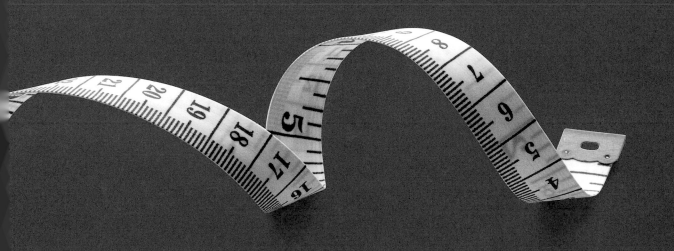

342
CALORIES
PER SERVING

classic pulled pork

SERVES 6
PREP: 10 MINUTES, PLUS MARINATING OVERNIGHT
HIGH 5–6 HOURS
LOW 8–10 HOURS

1kg boneless pork shoulder (with rind)
1 medium onion
6 small soft white or brown bread rolls (each around 55g)
mixed lettuce leaves
4 tomatoes
barbecue sauce or tomato relish, to serve (optional)

FOR THE RUB
2 tbsp soft light brown sugar
1 tbsp smoked paprika (not hot smoked)
2 tsp flaked sea salt
1 tsp garlic powder (see Tip below)
1 tsp coarsely ground black pepper

Tip: If you can't get hold of garlic powder, use four lightly crushed garlic cloves in the rub instead. If serving with a barbecue sauce or tomato relish, don't forget to add the extra calories.

I reckon slow cookers make the best pulled pork, as the long cooking and gentle heat softens the meat while leaving it really succulent. Pork shoulder is a fatty cut, but the fat gives the meat flavour. I've cut off the rind and much of the fat to keep the calories as low as possible without compromising the taste. Look out for small baps or rolls and stuff them with lots of salad, too.

To make the rub, put the sugar, paprika, salt, garlic powder and black pepper in a large, sturdy freezer bag and shake them around until well combined.

Snip off any string holding the pork together then carefully cut off the rind and fat. Peel and roughly chop the onion. Add the pork and onion into the rub and move them around in the bag until they are well coated. Seal the bag and put it in the fridge for several hours or overnight.

The next day, transfer the pork and its marinade to the slow cooker, cover with the lid and cook on HIGH for 5–6 hours or LOW for 8–10 hours, or until the pork is very soft and falls apart when prodded with a fork.

Remove the lid and shred the meat into the cooking juices with two forks. Serve the pulled pork from the slow cooker pot, on the table, with small rolls, lettuce, sliced tomatoes and barbecue sauce or tomato relish.

337

mexican pulled pork tacos

SERVES 6

PREP: 15 MINUTES, PLUS MARINATING OVERNIGHT

**HIGH 5-6 HOURS
LOW 8-10 HOURS**

1kg boneless pork shoulder (with rind)
12 corn tacos
2 little gem lettuces, or coleslaw (see below)
soured cream or half-fat crème fraiche, and lime wedges, to serve

FOR THE MARINADE
1 medium red onion
4 garlic cloves
1 orange
2 limes
1–2 tsp hot pepper sauce (from a bottle), or to taste
1 tbsp white wine vinegar or cider vinegar
1 tbsp soft light brown sugar
2 tsp dried oregano
1 tsp ground allspice
1 tsp ground cumin
1 tsp ground coriander
1 tsp flaked sea salt
1 tsp coarsely ground black pepper

Tip: Choose a Mexican-style chilli sauce made with habanero peppers if you can. Any leftover Mexican pork can be used for perking up a salad or rolled into wraps. It's also great reheated and tossed through savoury rice.

Soft, succulent and spicy, this Mexican-style pulled pork is fantastic piled into warm tacos with shredded lettuce or coleslaw, and makes a great alternative to burgers at a party. Heat the tacos on a baking tray in a warm oven for a few minutes before serving.

To make the marinade, peel and roughly chop the onion, peel and crush the garlic cloves, and cut the orange and limes in half and squeeze out the juice. Put the onion, garlic and citrus juice into a large, sturdy freezer bag. Holding the bag upright, add the remaining marinade ingredients and squish them around until well combined.

Snip off any string holding the pork together, then carefully cut off the rind and fat. Add the pork to the marinade and move it around in the bag until it is well coated. Seal the bag and put it in the fridge for several hours or overnight.

The next day, transfer the pork and its marinade to the slow cooker, cover with the lid and cook on HIGH for 5–6 hours or LOW for 8–10 hours, or until the pork is very soft and falls apart when prodded with a fork.

Remove the slow cooker lid and shred the meat into the cooking juices with two forks. Serve the pulled pork from the slow cooker pot, on the table, with warmed corn tacos, finely shredded lettuce or coleslaw (see below), soured cream or half-fat crème fraiche and a squeeze of fresh lime.

Crunchy coleslaw: Finely shred a quarter of a small red or white cabbage (about 250g), peel and coarsely grate 1 large carrot and thinly slice 4 spring onions. Put in a large bowl and add 100g soured cream and 4 tbsp mayonnaise. Season with pepper and mix well. Sprinkle with a few snipped fresh chives if you like. Serves 6. Calories per serving: 119

379
CALORIES
PER SERVING

somerset pork and apples

SERVES 3

PREP: 15 MINUTES

HIGH 3½–4½ HOURS,
PLUS 15 MINUTES

500g pork tenderloin (fillet)
1 medium onion
6–8 fresh sage leaves, plus
    extra to garnish
1 tbsp oil
250ml dry cider
100ml pork stock (made
    with ½ pork stock cube)
1 tsp soft light brown sugar
2 red-skinned eating apples
15g butter
2 tbsp cornflour
2 tbsp cold water
flaked sea salt
ground black pepper

Somerset pork and apples is one of the most popular recipes in my *Quick and Easy* cookbook, so I've developed a slow cooker version too. Pork tenderloin is very lean, so can dry out a little, but combining it with juicy apples and a rich cider sauce makes it taste totally delicious.

Trim the pork of any fat or sinew and cut it into roughly 1.5cm-thick slices. Season well with salt and pepper. Peel the onion, and thinly slice. Thinly slice the sage leaves. Heat half the oil in a large non-stick frying pan over a high heat. Fry the pork in batches for 1–2 minutes on each side until nicely coloured.

Transfer the pork to the slow cooker. Tip the onion and remaining oil into the same frying pan and cook over a medium heat for 3–4 minutes or until lightly browned, stirring occasionally. Add the onion to the pork and stir in the cider, stock, sugar and sage leaves. Season with a little salt and lots of freshly ground black pepper. Cover with the lid and cook on HIGH for 3½–4½ hours, or until the pork is tender.

Quarter the apples, remove the cores and cut into thick slices. Melt the butter in a non-stick frying pan and fry the apple slices over a medium heat for about 3–4 minutes or until golden brown and beginning to soften. Mix the cornflour and the water to a smooth paste.

Remove the slow cooker lid and stir the fried apple slices and cornflour mixture into the pork. Cover again and cook for a further 10 minutes, or until the sauce is thickened and glossy. Adjust the seasoning to taste and serve with lots of freshly cooked vegetables; shredded Savoy cabbage or kale and carrots go particularly well with the pork.

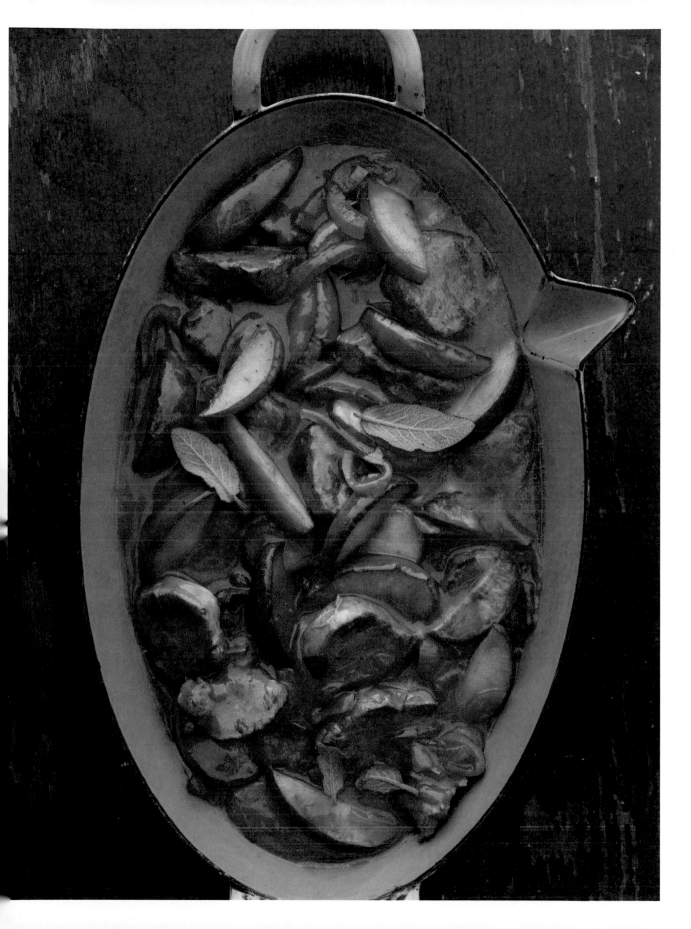

417
CALORIES
PER SERVING

sausage casserole

SERVES 4

PREP: 15 MINUTES

LOW 5–7 HOURS

2 tsp oil
12 good-quality pork
  chipolatas
2 medium red onions
½–1 tsp hot smoked paprika
  (depending on taste)
1 tsp ground cumin
1 tsp ground coriander
400g can red kidney beans
415g can baked beans
400g can chopped
  tomatoes
1 tsp mixed dried herbs
150ml just-boiled water
flaked sea salt
ground black pepper
fresh flat-leaf parsley,
  to garnish (optional)

Tip: Hot smoked paprika adds a lovely smoky barbecue flavour and some chilli heat, but you can use sweet smoked paprika instead if you don't want the casserole to be too spicy. It is labelled simply 'Smoked Paprika' in the supermarket.

Using chipolata sausages will make each serving of this family-friendly casserole feel more generous and allows you to serve between four and six people more easily. It doesn't take too long to prepare, so it's a great meal to bung in the slow cooker when you are planning to be out for a few hours and want something hot ready for your return.

Heat 1 teaspoon of the oil in a large non-stick frying pan and fry the chipolatas over a medium heat for 5 minutes or until browned on all sides. Transfer to the slow cooker.

While the sausages are browning, thinly slice the onions. Heat the remaining oil in the frying pan over a medium heat and cook the onions for 5 minutes, or until they begin to soften and lightly brown, stirring frequently. Sprinkle over the paprika, cumin and coriander and cook for a few seconds more, stirring continuously. Add to the sausages.

Rinse the kidney beans in a sieve under cold running water, then drain and stir into the sausage mixture with the baked beans, chopped tomatoes, herbs and water. Stir well then cover with the lid and cook on LOW for 5–7 hours, or until the sauce is thick and the spices have mellowed. Adjust the seasoning to taste and garnish with roughly chopped parsley, if using.

120
CALORIES
PER SERVING

honey roast ham

SERVES 16
**PREP: 10 MINUTES,
PLUS COOLING**
**HIGH 3½–4½ HOURS,
PLUS 15 MINUTES
LOW 5–7 HOURS,
PLUS 15 MINUTES**

1.4kg boneless, rolled
   smoked or unsmoked
   gammon
100ml water
1 tbsp prepared English
   mustard (from a jar)
1 tbsp clear honey

Decent-quality sliced ham is expensive to buy, but very easy to make if you have a slow cooker. Uncooked smoked and unsmoked gammon is often on offer at the supermarket and once you have cooked your ham, it should keep well for up to 3 days in the fridge, giving you the option of a host of different meals.

Put the gammon and water in the slow cooker, cover with the lid and cook on HIGH for 3½–4½ hours or LOW for 5–7 hours, or until the gammon is thoroughly cooked and reaches an internal temperature of at least 75°C.

Remove the lid, lift the gammon out of the slow cooker and on to a board, and leave it to stand for 10 minutes. Preheat the oven to 220°C/Fan 200°C/Gas 7. Very carefully snip off the string and slide a knife under the rind, then lift it off, leaving a thin layer of fat on the meat. Score the fat with a knife in a crisscross pattern.

Line a small roasting tin with a piece of foil, large enough to come up the sides of the tin. Place the ham on top. Mix the mustard and honey in a small bowl and spread it all over the ham fat. Bring the foil in towards the ham to create a bowl to catch any sticky juices. Bake the ham for about 15 minutes, or until nicely browned. Serve in slices, warm or cold.

488
CALORIES
PER SERVING

sticky pork ribs

SERVES 4

PREP: 5 MINUTES

**HIGH 3-4 HOURS,
PLUS 30 MINUTES
LOW 5-7 HOURS,
PLUS 30 MINUTES ON HIGH**

900g pork spare ribs

FOR THE GLAZE
1 garlic clove
1 long red chilli (optional)
75g tomato ketchup
3 tbsp dark soy sauce
2 tbsp clear honey

This is a really fab recipe for anyone who loves Chinese-style pork ribs. They are incredibly easy to make in the slow cooker and turn out perfectly succulent and sticky every time. Pork ribs are cheap but fairly high in calories, so keep these for an occasional rather than a regular meal.

Put the pork ribs in the slow cooker. Cover with the lid and cook on HIGH for 3–4 hours or LOW for 5–7 hours, or until the meat is very tender.

For the glaze, peel and crush the garlic, and finely dice the chilli (if using). Mix them with the ketchup, soy sauce and honey. Remove the slow cooker lid and carefully drain off and discard any fat or cooking liquor from the ribs. (You will probably need to remove the ribs first and then return them to the pot.)

Pour the sauce over the ribs and gently turn to coat them. Cover with the lid and cook on HIGH for a further 30 minutes, or until the sauce is thick and glossy and the meat is falling off the bones. Transfer to a warmed platter and serve with a massive salad.

138
CALORIES
PER SERVING

pulled ham

SERVES 12
PREP: 10 MINUTES
HIGH 5–6 HOURS
LOW 8–10 HOURS

1.4kg boneless, rolled
   smoked or unsmoked
   gammon
100ml water

Pulled ham is a convenient ingredient to have in the fridge as it can be used for salads, sandwiches, pasta dishes, omelettes and quiche fillings, and even bunged into lentil and pea soup. Gammon is relatively cheap to buy and once you've trimmed off all the rind and fat, can be quite lean. What's more, it should keep well for up to 3 days in the fridge.

Put the gammon and water in the slow cooker, cover with the lid and cook on HIGH for 5–6 hours or LOW for 8–10 hours, or until the gammon is thoroughly cooked and falls apart when pressed with a fork.

Remove the slow cooker lid, lift the gammon out and transfer it to a board. Very carefully snip off the string and slide a knife under the rind and fat and lift them off.

Using two forks, break up the meat you are ready to eat by pulling the strands apart. Quickly cool any meat you aren't going to eat immediately, then put it in a freezer bag or on a covered plate and keep in the fridge. Take out and shred what you need when you need it. Eat within 3 days.

Ham and egg salad: Wash and separate the leaves from 2 little gem lettuces and place on a platter. Scatter a third of a cucumber, thinly sliced, and 12 halved cherry tomatoes on top. Add 4 halved hard-boiled eggs and 200g pulled ham. Drizzle with 3 tablespoons of salad cream mixed with 1 tablespoon of cold water and serve. Serves 4. Calories per serving: 202

222
CALORIES
PER SERVING

crustless quiche lorraine

SERVES 4

**PREP: 15 MINUTES,
PLUS COOLING**

LOW 1½-2 HOURS

1 small onion
1 small, slender leek
2 smoked back bacon
   rashers (about 70g)
1 tsp oil
25g Gruyère or mature
   Cheddar cheese
3 large eggs, plus 2 large
   egg yolks
150ml semi-skimmed milk
ground black pepper

Tip: You can use ham
instead of bacon for the
filling (about 50g) if you
like, torn or cut into strips.

Use an oval slow cooker
with a 3.5-litre or larger
capacity to cook this
quiche.

Cutting the pastry out of a quiche recipe drastically reduces the calories. And cooking it in a slow cooker means you can make a lighter egg filling without worrying that it is going to separate. This quiche makes a delicious light lunch or supper, served with a large mixed salad. Use a foil loaf tin if you don't have a metal one the right size.

Line the base of a 450g foil or metal loaf tin with baking parchment or use a ready-made parchment cake liner. The tin will need to be roughly 7cm x 17cm across the base. Peel and thinly slice the onion and trim and thinly slice the leek. Trim the fat off the bacon and cut the bacon into short, roughly 1cm-wide strips.

Heat the oil in a large non-stick frying pan and gently fry the onion, leek and bacon together for 4–5 minutes or until beginning to lightly brown, stirring frequently. Spread over the base of the lined tin. Coarsely grate the cheese and sprinkle it over the top of the onions, leeks and bacon.

Whisk the eggs and egg yolks together with a metal whisk until well combined. Stir the milk into the eggs and season with pepper. Pour over the cheese, bacon and vegetables. Cover the top of the tin with foil and pinch around the edges to seal.

Place two upturned ramekins in the slow cooker and put the loaf tin on top. This will raise the tin so it fits better. Pour enough just-boiled water to come 5cm up the sides of the slow cooker pot. Cover with the lid and cook on LOW for 1½–2 hours, or until set.

Carefully remove the tin from the slow cooker, holding it with an oven cloth. Remove the foil lid and leave it to cool on the work surface for 30 minutes. Turn it out of the tin and serve just warm in thick slices or triangles. Keep any leftovers well covered in the fridge.

526
CALORIES
PER SERVING

spicy pork pilaf

SERVES 4

PREP TIME: 15 MINUTES

HIGH 3–4 HOURS, PLUS 30 MINUTES

LOW 5–7 HOURS, PLUS 30 MINUTES ON HIGH

1 medium onion
2 garlic cloves
50g soft cooking chorizo (from the chiller cabinet)
1 tbsp olive oil
500g pork shoulder steaks
1 tsp ground cumin
1 tsp ground coriander
½ tsp hot chilli powder
500ml hot chicken or pork stock (made with 1 chicken or pork stock cube)
1 red and 1 orange or yellow pepper
100g green beans
150g easy-cook long-grain rice
flaked sea salt
ground black pepper

Pork shoulder steak is a great value cut that cooks well in a slow cooker. Once nice and tender, rice and vegetables can be added to make a very satisfying and delicious one-pot meal. You can swap the shoulder for lean tenderloin (fillet) if you prefer, but bear in mind that the meat won't be quite as succulent.

Peel and slice the onion into thin wedges, and peel and crush the garlic. Cut the chorizo into roughly 1cm-thick slices. Heat the oil in a large, non-stick frying pan and fry the onion wedges over a medium-high heat for 3–5 minutes, or until softened and lightly browned, stirring frequently.

While the onion is cooking, trim excess fat from the pork steaks and cut them into roughly 2.5cm chunks. Season with a little salt and pepper and add to the pan. Fry with the onion for 2–3 minutes until lightly browned, then add the garlic and spices and cook for 30 seconds more, stirring continuously. Transfer to the slow cooker.

Pour a little of the stock into the frying pan and let it bubble for a few seconds, stirring to lift any tasty sediment from the bottom of the pan, then pour it over the pork and onion. Add the remaining stock and chorizo, stir well, cover with the lid and cook on HIGH for 3–4 hours or LOW for 5–7 hours, or until the pork is very tender.

Deseed and thinly slice the peppers and trim the green beans, cutting any particularly long beans in half. Remove the slow cooker lid and add the peppers, beans and rice to the pork and onion. Stir well then cover again and cook on HIGH for a further 30 minutes, or until the liquid has been absorbed and the rice and vegetables are tender.

meat-free

203

CALORIES
PER SERVING

vegetable frittata

SERVES 4

**PREP: 15 MINUTES,
PLUS COOLING**

LOW 1½ –2½ HOURS

1 small onion
1 garlic clove
1 red and 1 yellow pepper
1 tbsp olive oil
50g frozen peas
5 large eggs
2 tbsp semi-skimmed milk
2 tbsp cornflour
flaked sea salt
ground black pepper

Tip: Use an oval slow cooker with a 3.5-litre or larger capacity to cook this frittata. If yours is smaller, try making it in parchment-lined ramekins instead and reduce the cooking time to 1½ –2 hours.

This is an easy vegetable-packed frittata – like a thick Spanish omelette – that can be cut into squares or triangles and kept in the fridge. Cooking the frittata in the slow cooker means it won't curdle or burn and it's perfect for a light lunch served with a mixed salad, or eaten as a healthy snack.

Line the base of a 450g foil or metal loaf tin with baking parchment or a cake liner. The tin will need to be roughly 7cm x 17cm across the base. Peel and thinly slice the onion and peel and crush the garlic. Deseed and thinly slice the peppers.

Heat the oil in a large non-stick frying pan and fry the onion and peppers together for 6–8 minutes or until softened and starting to lightly brown, stirring frequently. Add the garlic and peas and cook for a further 30–60 seconds, or until the peas are thawed, stirring continuously. Tip all the vegetables into the prepared tin.

Whisk the eggs together with a metal whisk until well combined. Mix the cornflour with the milk until smooth, then stir into the eggs and season with salt and pepper. Pour over the vegetables. Cover the top of the tin with foil and pinch around the edges to seal. (This will prevent water dripping on the frittata.)

Place two upturned ramekins in the slow cooker and put the loaf tin on top. This will raise the tin so it fits better. Pour in enough just-boiled water from a kettle to come 5cm up the sides of the slow cooker pot. Cover with the lid and cook on LOW for 1½–2½ hours, or until firm.

Carefully remove the tin, holding it with an oven cloth. Remove the foil and turn out the frittata onto a chopping board. Serve warm or cold in thick slices or triangles. Keep any leftovers well covered in the fridge.

398
CALORIES
PER SERVING

sweet potato and root vegetable hot pot

SERVES 4

PREP: 15 MINUTES

HIGH 4-5 HOURS
LOW 6-8 HOURS

2 medium onions
1 tbsp oil
3-4 medium sweet potatoes
    (about 800g)
3 medium carrots
    (about 300g)
2 medium parsnips
    (about 250g)
3 tbsp plain flour (25g)
2 tbsp tomato purée
2 tsp dried mixed herbs
400ml hot vegetable stock
    (made with 1 vegetable
    stock cube)
400g can butterbeans
400g can chopped
    tomatoes
½ tsp dried chilli flakes
    (optional)
flaked sea salt
ground black pepper
fresh flat-leaf parsley, to
    serve (optional)
fresh basil pesto, to serve
    (optional)

Freeze the cooked and cooled hotpot in labelled zip-seal bags or freezer-proof containers for up to 4 months. Thaw overnight in the fridge and reheat in the microwave or a large saucepan over a medium heat, stirring occasionally, until piping hot.

A really fab vegetable dish that's full of flavour and very filling. It's also relatively low in calories but high in fibre due to all the lovely vegetables and beans. Serve as a one-pot meal with a spoonful of fresh basil pesto, or as a vegetable accompaniment to some grilled meat or fish. You can even whizz up any leftovers to make a delicious soup.

Peel and thinly slice the onions. Pour the oil into a large non-stick frying pan and fry the onions over a medium-high heat for 5 minutes, or until softened and lightly browned, stirring occasionally.

While the onions are cooking, peel the sweet potatoes and cut them into roughly 3cm chunks. Peel the carrots and parsnips and cut into roughly 3cm chunks. Put the onions and other vegetables into the slow cooker, add the flour and season with a little salt and plenty of pepper. Toss well together.

Mix the tomato purée and herbs with the hot vegetable stock and pour over the vegetables. Rinse the butterbeans in a sieve under cold running water, and drain. Add the beans, canned tomatoes and chilli, if using, to the slow cooker and stir well. Cover with the lid and cook on HIGH for 4-5 hours or LOW for 6-8 hours, or until all the vegetables are tender and the sauce is thick. Remove the slow cooker lid and scatter with freshly chopped parsley and add a spoonful of pesto, if using, just before serving.

233

veggie bean chilli

SERVES 4
PREP: 10-12 MINUTES
HIGH 2-3 HOURS
LOW 4-6 HOURS

2 medium onions
2 garlic cloves
1 tbsp oil
½ tsp dried chilli flakes
1 tsp ground cumin
1 tsp ground coriander
½ tsp ground cinnamon
150ml hot vegetable stock
    (made with 1 vegetable
    stock cube)
400g can chopped
    tomatoes
395g can red kidney beans
    in chilli sauce
1 tsp mixed dried herbs
400g can mixed beans
flaked sea salt
ground black pepper

Freeze the cooked and
cooled chilli in labelled
zip-seal bags or freezer-
proof containers for up to
3 months. Thaw overnight in
the fridge and reheat in the
microwave or in a large
saucepan over a medium
heat, stirring frequently,
until piping hot.

A warming supper that all the family can enjoy. Serve with
cooked rice, topped with natural yoghurt and fresh coriander,
or flatbreads and salad with soured cream and a little grated
cheese. You'll find my recipe for easy yoghurt flatbreads
below, but you can use warmed mini tortillas instead if you like
– just don't forget to add the extra calories.

Peel and thinly slice the onions and peel and crush the garlic.
Heat the oil in a large non-stick frying pan and fry the onions
for 5 minutes, or until softened and lightly browned, stirring
frequently. Add the garlic, chilli flakes, cumin, coriander and
cinnamon and cook for a further minute.

Transfer to the slow cooker. Stir in the stock, canned tomatoes,
red kidney beans in chilli sauce and dried herbs. Drain the
mixed beans in a sieve and rinse under cold running water.
Add to the slow cooker and season with salt and pepper.

Stir well then cover with the lid and cook on HIGH for 2–3 hours
or LOW for 4–6 hours, or until the sauce is thick and the spices
have mellowed. If you get a chance, stir the chilli halfway
through the cooking time, quickly replacing the lid.

Yoghurt flatbreads: Mix 200g self-raising flour, ¼ teaspoon of
fine sea salt, 100g low-fat natural yoghurt and 3 tablespoons of
cold water to make a soft, pliable dough. Knead briefly then
divide into 4 portions and roll out on a lightly floured surface
until about 5mm thick. Place a large non-stick frying pan over a
high heat. Cook the flatbreads one at a time for 1½–2 minutes
on each side, or until lightly browned. Serve warm with the
chilli. Makes 4. Calories per flatbread: 179

234

chickpea and bean masala

SERVES 4

PREP: 20 MINUTES

HIGH 3-4 HOURS,
PLUS 5 MINUTES
LOW 6-8 HOURS,
PLUS 5 MINUTES

2 medium onions
1 tbsp oil
2 garlic cloves
25g chunk of fresh root
    ginger
1 long green chilli (deseeded
    first if you like)
2 tbsp medium curry
    powder
400g can chopped
    tomatoes
400g can chickpeas
400g can mixed beans
2 medium carrots (about
    200g)
½ tsp flaked sea salt, plus
    extra to season
1 tsp caster sugar
100g young spinach leaves
ground black pepper
minted yoghurt (see page
    45), to serve
warmed flatbreads (see
    page 101), to serve

Freeze the cooked and
cooled curry in labelled
zip-seal bags or freezer-
proof containers for up to
3 months. Defrost in
the fridge overnight and
reheat thoroughly in the
microwave or a large
saucepan over a medium
heat, stirring gently, until
piping hot.

This chickpea curry is the sort of thing you can rustle up easily using store cupboard ingredients. It's worth frying the onions for just 5 minutes before adding them to the slow cooker, as they will bring a richness to the dish that would otherwise be lacking. Serve with yoghurt flatbreads (page 101) for a healthy feast, or as an accompaniment – this quantity will make 6 smaller servings containing 156 calories.

Peel and thinly slice the onions. Heat the oil in a large non-stick frying pan and fry the onions for 5 minutes over a medium-high heat, or until softened and lightly browned, stirring occasionally.

While the onions are cooking, peel and crush the garlic, peel and finely grate the root ginger and finely chop the chilli. Add to the pan and cook with the onions for a further minute, stirring. Sprinkle over the curry powder and cook for a few seconds, stirring constantly, then scrape all the cooked vegetables into the slow cooker.

Tip the canned tomatoes on top. Rinse the chickpeas and beans in a sieve under cold running water, then drain. Add to the slow cooker. Half-fill one of the cans with water and pour it on top (you'll need about 200ml). Peel the carrots and cut into roughly 1cm chunks.

Add the carrots, salt and sugar to the other vegetables and beans. Season with a little pepper and stir well. Cover with the lid and cook on HIGH for 3-4 hours or LOW for 6-8 hours, or until the vegetables and pulses are very tender and the sauce is thick. When the curry is ready, remove the slow cooker lid and stir in the spinach leaves, a handful at a time. Cover again and cook for a further 3-5 minutes, or until the spinach has softened.

Remove the lid, season the curry with salt and pepper to taste and serve with warm flatbreads or small portions of basmati rice and minted yoghurt.

388

CALORIES
PER SERVING

paneer and vegetable curry

SERVES 4

PREP: 20 MINUTES

HIGH 4-5 HOURS,
PLUS 10 MINUTES

LOW 6-8 HOURS,
PLUS 10 MINUTES

2 medium onions
3 garlic cloves
25g chunk of fresh root
    ginger
1 long green chilli (deseeded
    first if you like)
400g potatoes (ideally
    Maris Piper)
1 tbsp oil
1 tsp cumin seeds
1 tbsp medium curry
    powder
2 tbsp plain flour
400g can chopped
    tomatoes
500ml hot vegetable stock
    (made with 1 vegetable
    stock cube)
100g young spinach leaves
100g frozen peas (thawed)
225g paneer (from the
    chiller cabinet)
1 tsp caster sugar (optional)
flaked sea salt
ground black pepper
warmed yoghurt flatbreads
    (see page 101) or cooked
    rice, to serve

Flat-freeze the cooked and
cooled curry in labelled zip-
seal bags for up to 1 month.
Reheat thoroughly from
frozen in the microwave or
a large saucepan over a
medium heat, stirring
frequently, until piping hot.

**Paneer is an Indian cheese that cooks beautifully and retains
its texture. You'll need to add it once the vegetable curry is
ready, as it only takes a couple of minutes to cook.**

Peel and thinly slice the onions, peel and crush the garlic, peel
and finely grate the ginger and finely chop the green chilli. Peel
the potatoes and cut them into roughly 2cm chunks.

Heat 2 teaspoons of the oil in a large non-stick frying pan over a
medium-high heat and fry the cumin seeds for a few seconds,
stirring. Add the onions and cook for 5 minutes or until lightly
browned, stirring frequently.

Add the garlic, ginger, green chilli and curry powder and cook
for a further 1-2 minutes, stirring continuously. Transfer to the
slow cooker and toss with the flour. Add the potatoes, canned
tomatoes and stock. Stir well, cover with the lid and cook on
HIGH for 4-5 hours or LOW for 6-8 hours, until the vegetables
are tender and the spices have mellowed.

Once the curry is ready, remove the slow cooker lid and stir in
the spinach leaves, a handful at a time, followed by the peas.
Cover again and cook for a further 5 minutes. Meanwhile, cut
the paneer into roughly 2cm cubes. Brush the remaining
teaspoon of oil over a large non-stick frying pan and fry the
paneer for 2-3 minutes, turning frequently until the cubes are
lightly browned.

Check the curry seasoning - you may want a little extra salt
or pepper and sugar for a touch of sweetness - then add the
warm paneer cubes and serve with flatbreads or rice.

216
CALORIES
PER SERVING

sicilian aubergine and bean stew

SERVES 4
PREP: 20 MINUTES
HIGH 3–4 HOURS,
PLUS 30 MINUTES
LOW 5–7 HOURS,
PLUS 30 MINUTES ON HIGH

1 large red onion
3 slender celery sticks
oil, for spraying
3 garlic cloves
1 tsp coriander seeds
400g can chopped
    tomatoes
400g can cannellini beans
2 tbsp tomato purée
200ml cold water
40g soft light brown sugar
75ml red wine or extra cold
    water
2 tbsp baby capers (from a
    jar), drained (optional)
1 tbsp red wine vinegar
2 medium aubergines
    (about 225g each)
1 tbsp pine nuts (10g)
flaked sea salt
ground black pepper
1 tbsp extra virgin olive oil
fresh basil leaves, to serve

Freeze the cooked and
cooled stew in labelled zip-
seal bags or freezer-proof
containers for up to
3 months. Thaw overnight
in the fridge and reheat in
a large saucepan or the
microwave, stirring
frequently, until piping hot.

This slow-cooked aubergine stew really benefits from the gentle cooking of the tangy tomato sauce. Serve warm, or at room temperature, with a salad and some crusty bread. If taking straight from the fridge, allow to return to room temperature for 30–60 minutes before serving.

Peel and thinly slice the onion and trim and thinly slice the celery. Place a large non-stick frying pan over a medium-high heat and spray with oil. Add the onions and celery and cook for 5 minutes, stirring occasionally.

Peel and very thinly slice the garlic and lightly crush the coriander seeds in a pestle and mortar or with the end of a rolling pin. Add the garlic and coriander to the onion and celery and cook for a further 30 seconds, stirring frequently. Put into the slow cooker.

Tip the chopped tomatoes into the slow cooker. Rinse the cannellini beans in a sieve under cold running water, and drain. Add the cannellini beans, tomato purée, water, sugar, wine or extra water, capers and vinegar to the slow cooker and season with a pinch of salt and plenty of pepper. Stir well then cover with the lid and cook on HIGH for 3–4 hours or LOW for 5–7 hours, or until the sauce is rich and thick.

Cut the aubergines into roughly 3cm chunks. Spray a large non-stick frying pan or wok with oil and place over a medium-high heat. Add half the aubergines, season with salt and pepper and spray with more oil. Fry for 3–4 minutes or until lightly browned all over, stirring frequently. Tip on to a plate.

Repeat with the remaining aubergines. Add all the aubergines to the slow cooker and stir well. Cover and cook on HIGH for a further 30–45 minutes or until the aubergines are very tender. Remove the lid, stir in the pine nuts and adjust the seasoning to taste.

Serve warm, or leave to cool, then cover and keep in the fridge and eat within 3 days. Drizzle with the extra virgin olive oil and garnish with basil leaves to serve.

215
CALORIES
PER SERVING

slow veggie bolognese

SERVES 6
PREP: 20 MINUTES
HIGH 4–5 HOURS
LOW 8–10 HOURS

1 medium onion
2 garlic cloves
2 medium carrots
1 medium courgette
1 red pepper
150g portobello or chestnut
    mushrooms
150g dried puy lentils
150g dried red split lentils
400g can chopped
    tomatoes
600ml hot vegetable stock
    (made with 1 vegetable
    stock cube)
2 tbsp tomato purée
1 tsp dried oregano or
    mixed dried herbs
1 bay leaf
flaked sea salt
ground black pepper

Flat-freeze the cooked and
cooled Bolognese sauce in
labelled zip-seal bags for up
to 4 months. Reheat
thoroughly from frozen in
the microwave or a large
saucepan over a medium
heat, stirring frequently,
until piping hot.

Tip: You can also use a
250g sachet of pre-cooked
puy lentils for this recipe,
but you'll need to reduce
the stock to 250ml.

This rich, high-fibre veggie Bolognese uses lots of vegetables and lentils. It makes four really generous servings or six smaller portions. It freezes very well and can be used for a lasagne, pasta bake or base for veggie cottage pie; perfect if you like to go meat-free or simply fancy a change.

Peel and finely chop the onion, peel and crush the garlic, peel and finely grate the carrots, finely grate the courgette, deseed and finely dice the pepper and roughly chop the mushrooms. Put all the vegetables in the slow cooker.

Put the lentils in a sieve and rinse under cold water, then drain. Add to the slow cooker along with the canned tomatoes, stock, tomato purée and herbs. Season with salt and plenty of pepper. (If you are leaving the Bolognese to cook longer than 8 hours, add an extra 100ml cold water to the pot.) Mix really well to combine the ingredients thoroughly.

Cover with the lid and cook on HIGH for 4–5 hours or LOW for 8–10 hours, or until the vegetables and lentils are soft. If you get a chance, stir the Bolognese halfway through the cooking time, quickly replacing the lid. Adjust the seasoning to taste and add a little extra just-boiled water if necessary, before serving.

308
CALORIES
PER SERVING

sweet potato dhal

SERVES 4

PREP: 15 MINUTES

HIGH 3–4 HOURS
LOW 5–7 HOURS

1 medium onion
2 garlic cloves
2–3 large sweet potatoes
   (about 500g)
1 tbsp oil
1 tbsp medium curry
   powder
200g dried red split lentils
1 tsp flaked sea salt,
   plus extra to season
750ml water
1–2 tbsp fresh lime or lemon
   juice, to taste
ground black pepper
low-fat natural yoghurt and
   lime or lemon wedges,
   to serve

Freeze the cooked and
cooled dhal in labelled
freezer-proof containers for
up to 3 months. Thaw
overnight then add a splash
more water and reheat in a
large non-stick saucepan
over a medium heat, or in the
microwave, until piping hot.

This lightly curried dhal makes a brilliant lunch or light
supper, served with natural yoghurt and flatbreads. Packed
in a suitable container, it can be warmed up at work, too.
Alternatively, serve it alongside another curry to make
the meal go further.

Peel and thinly slice the onion and peel and crush the garlic.
Peel and cut the sweet potatoes into roughly 3cm chunks.

Heat the oil in a large non-stick frying pan and fry the onion
over a medium heat for 5 minutes or until softened and very
lightly browned, stirring frequently, adding the garlic for the
last minute of cooking time. Stir in the curry powder and cook
for a few seconds more. Transfer to the slow cooker.

Rinse the lentils in a sieve under cold running water then drain
and add to the pot. Stir in the sweet potatoes, salt and water.
Cover with the lid and cook on HIGH for 3–4 hours or LOW for
5–7 hours, or until the lentils and sweet potato are very tender.
Stir the dhal roughly halfway through the cooking time if you
get a chance, quickly replacing the lid.

Take the pot carefully out of the slow-cooker base and beat the
lentils and sweet potatoes with a wooden spoon until they
blend to make an almost smooth dhal. Stir in the lime or lemon
juice and adjust the seasoning to taste. Top with spiced
shallots, if you like (see recipe below).

Golden spiced shallots: Peel and thinly slice 3 long shallots or
1 medium onion. Heat 1 tablespoon of oil in a non-stick frying
pan and fry for 5 minutes, or until nicely browned. Add ½
teaspoon each of lightly crushed coriander and cumin seeds
and a little pepper, and cook for a few seconds more. Spoon over
the dhal just before serving. Serves 4. Calories per serving: 38

317

slow squash risotto

SERVES 4

PREP: 15 MINUTES

**HIGH 3–4 HOURS,
PLUS 35 MINUTES**

1 small-medium butternut
    squash (about 750g)
1 medium onion
1 tbsp olive oil
1 garlic clove
150g Arborio (risotto) rice
50ml Marsala, Madeira or
    extra vegetable stock
650ml hot vegetable stock
    (made with 1 vegetable
    stock cube)
100g young spinach leaves
50g Parmesan or Grana
    Padano cheese
flaked sea salt
ground black pepper

Tip: Check with the
manufacturer's instructions
to make sure that your slow
cooker is suitable for cooking
without added liquid.

A risotto made in a slow cooker won't be quite as creamy-tasting as a traditional risotto, as it isn't stirred continuously to release the starch. Nevertheless, this is a handy and healthy one-pot dish that also reheats well the next day.

Peel the squash with a good vegetable peeler then cut it in half lengthways, scoop out the seeds and cut it into roughly 3cm chunks. Peel and finely chop the onion and put the squash and onion into the slow cooker.

Add the oil, salt to season and a good grind of black pepper and toss well together. Cover with the lid and cook on HIGH for 3–4 hours, or until the squash is tender and the onion is nicely browned.

Peel and crush the garlic, remove the slow cooker lid and stir the garlic, rice and Marsala or Madeira (if using) into the vegetables. Pour over the stock and stir well, making sure the rice is fully submerged in the stock, then cover again and cook for a further 30–40 minutes, or until the rice is tender.

Remove the lid, stir in the spinach leaves, a handful at a time, then grate the Parmesan or Grana Padano and add to the risotto. Stir well then cover with the lid and cook for a further 2–3 minutes or until the spinach is soft. Serve with a mixed salad.

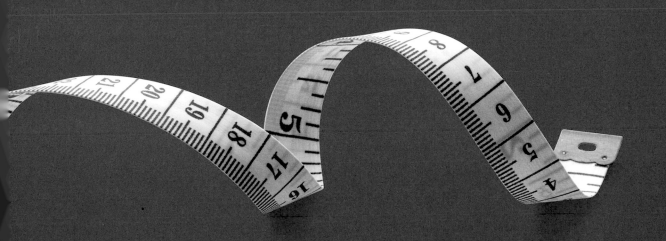

fish and
seafood

463
CALORIES
PER SERVING

easy fish with chorizo

SERVES 2
PREP: 10 MINUTES
HIGH 1½-2 HOURS,
PLUS 20 MINUTES

1 orange or yellow pepper
1 medium red onion
1 large courgette
50g soft cooking chorizo
    (from the chiller cabinet)
200g cherry tomatoes
1 tbsp extra virgin olive oil
2 tbsp cold water
400g can chickpeas
2 x 150g fresh skinless white
    fish fillets, such as cod or
    haddock
a few thyme sprigs
    (optional)
flaked sea salt
ground black pepper

This is a lovely, easy dish that's perfect if you aren't a confident cook but want to try your hand at cooking fish. The combination of chorizo sausage and fish works surprisingly well, so don't be afraid to give it a go.

Deseed the pepper and cut it into roughly 3cm chunks, then peel and cut the red onion into very thin rings. Trim the courgette, halve lengthways and cut it into roughly 2cm slices. Cut the chorizo into roughly 5mm slices.

Put the pepper, onion, courgette, chorizo and tomatoes into the slow cooker, add the olive oil and water and lightly toss. Season the vegetables with black pepper and a pinch of salt, cover with the lid and cook on HIGH for 1½–2 hours, or until almost tender.

Rinse the chickpeas in a sieve under cold running water, and drain. Remove the slow cooker lid, stir the chickpeas into the vegetables and place the fish fillets on top. Season the fish with ground black pepper. Add a few fresh thyme leaves if you like.

Cover again and cook for a further 20–30 minutes, or until the chickpeas are hot and the fish is cooked and beginning to flake (this will depend on the thickness of your fillets). Transfer the fish and vegetables to two warmed plates and spoon over the lovely cooking juices. Garnish with some more fresh thyme, if you like.

473
CALORIES
PER SERVING

paella

SERVES 4

PREP: 20 MINUTES

HIGH 1½-2 HOURS,
PLUS 40 MINUTES

6 boneless, skinless chicken
   thighs (500g)
50g soft cooking chorizo
   (from the chiller cabinet)
1 medium onion
1 red and 1 yellow pepper
100g fine green beans
2 garlic cloves
1 tbsp olive oil
1-2 tsp hot smoked paprika
good pinch of saffron
   threads
1 fresh bay leaf or 2 dried
   bay leaves
150g uncoated squid rings,
   thawed if frozen
300ml hot stock (made
   with 1 chicken or fish
   stock cube)
150g paella rice
250g cooked, peeled king
   prawns, thawed if frozen
flaked sea salt
ground black pepper
fresh flat-leaf parsley, to
   garnish (optional)
lemon wedges, for
   squeezing

A simple combination of seafood with chicken, chorizo and
rice. If you can't find uncoated squid rings, use the cones
instead and cut into roughly 1cm slices. Serve the paella with a
large mixed salad dressed with a mustardy vinaigrette, and
lemon wedges for squeezing.

Trim any excess fat off the chicken thighs with kitchen scissors
and cut each thigh in half. Cut the chorizo into roughly 1cm-
thick slices. Peel and finely chop the onion and deseed and
thickly slice the peppers. Trim the green beans and cut them
into roughly 3cm lengths, and peel and crush the garlic.

Heat the oil in a large non-stick frying pan over a medium heat.
Season the chicken thighs with salt and pepper and fry for
3–5 minutes, turning once, until lightly browned. Add the
chorizo to the pan and cook for a further 30 seconds, turning
once. Transfer the chicken and chorizo to the slow cooker,
leaving the fat in the pan.

Add the onion to the frying pan and fry gently for 4–5 minutes
or until softened and very lightly browned, stirring occasionally.
Stir in the garlic, smoked paprika, saffron and bay leaf and cook
for 30 seconds more, stirring continuously. Add the spiced
onions and squid to the chicken.

Pour over the stock, season with pepper and stir well. Place the
peppers and green beans on top. Cover with the lid and cook
on HIGH for 1½–2 hours, or until the chicken is tender and
thoroughly cooked.

Remove the slow cooker lid, and stir in the rice, making sure it is
submerged in the stock. Cover and cook for 30 minutes more,
or until the rice is tender. Add the prawns to the paella, stir well,
and cover again. Cook for a further 8–10 minutes, or until the
prawns are hot throughout. Serve sprinked with parsley and
lemon wedges for squeezing.

214
CALORIES
PER SERVING

hearty fish stew

SERVES 4
PREP: 15 MINUTES
HIGH 3-4 HOURS,
PLUS 15 MINUTES
LOW 4-6 HOURS,
PLUS 15 MINUTES ON HIGH

250ml just-boiled water
1 fish stock cube
good pinch of saffron
    threads
1 tsp fennel seeds
1 medium onion
2 garlic cloves
1 medium fennel bulb
    (about 250g)
1 tbsp olive oil
½ tsp dried chilli flakes
1 tsp dried oregano
1 fresh bay leaf or 2 dried
    bay leaves
400g can chopped
    tomatoes
50ml white wine
good pinch flaked sea salt
300g potatoes (ideally
    Maris Piper)
400g fresh thick, skinless
    white fish fillet, such as
    cod or haddock
ground black pepper
fresh flat-leaf parsley, to
    garnish (optional)

The combination of tomatoes, fennel and potatoes makes a hearty soup base that can be left to simmer for several hours before the fish is added. After a final 15 minutes cooking the dish is ready.

Pour the just-boiled water into a heat-proof jug, add the stock cube and stir until dissolved. Add the saffron and leave to stand for 10 minutes. Lightly crush the fennel seeds in a pestle and mortar.

Peel and thinly slice the onion and garlic. Trim and thinly slice the fennel lengthways. Heat the oil in a large non-stick frying pan and fry the onion and fennel for 5 minutes over a medium heat until they begin to soften and lightly brown, stirring frequently. Add the garlic, spices, oregano and bay leaf and cook for a few seconds more.

Tip into the slow cooker and add the chopped tomatoes, wine and salt. Peel the potatoes and cut them into roughly 3cm chunks. Add the chopped potatoes to the slow cooker, pour over the saffron and stock and stir well. Cover with the lid and cook on HIGH for 3-4 hours or LOW for 4-6 hours, or until the vegetables are tender. (The stew base can be cooled at this point, then reheated in a large saucepan on the hob before adding the fish, if you like.)

Cut the fish into roughly 4cm chunks. Remove the slow cooker lid and stir the fish into the tomato and fennel stew. Cover again and cook for 15-20 minutes more on HIGH, or until the fish is cooked. It should be just beginning to flake. (The cooking time will depend on the thickness of your fish pieces.) Scatter roughly chopped parsley over the top, if using, and serve in warmed, deep bowls.

372

lemon and parsley salmon

SERVES 6
PREP: 25 MINUTES
HIGH 1½–2½ HOURS

2 x 500g fillets fresh salmon
1 lemon
4 fresh bay leaves
200ml cold water
flaked sea salt
ground black pepper

FOR THE STUFFING
1 medium onion
1 large garlic clove
15g butter
1 tbsp oil
1 lemon
50g bunch of fresh flat-leaf
  parsley
40g dry white breadcrumbs
  or panko breadcrumbs

Most fish needs a short cooking time, but thick salmon fillet can be stuffed and tied then poached in a slow cooker very successfully. This is a great dish for a special supper or lunch, served with a few boiled new potatoes and freshly cooked vegetables or salad.

To make the stuffing, peel and finely chop the onion and peel and crush the garlic. Melt the butter with the oil in a large non-stick frying pan over a low heat, and cook the onion and garlic for 5 minutes, or until well softened but not coloured, stirring frequently.

Finely grate the zest from the lemon and squeeze the juice. Strip the parsley leaves off the stalks and finely chop. Remove the onion and garlic from the heat and add the lemon zest and juice, chopped parsley and breadcrumbs. Season with a couple of pinches of salt and lots of pepper. Place one of the salmon fillets on a large board, skin side down. Cut kitchen string into 3–4 lengths, each roughly 60cm long. Slide the string under the salmon until evenly spaced apart.

Season the salmon with a little ground black pepper. Spoon the stuffing all over the salmon and press down lightly. Season the second salmon fillet and place on top of the stuffing, skin side up. Thinly slice half the lemon. Bring the centre length of string up around the salmon and stuffing, place a slice of lemon and a bay leaf on top of the salmon and tie the string around it, securing it with a knot. Repeat with the remaining string, lemon slices and bay leaves. Trim the knots.

Gently lift the stuffed salmon and place it on a piece of foil. Fold the foil so it creates a neat parcel around the salmon and lift gently into the slow cooker. Add the water, cover with the lid and cook on HIGH for 1½–2½ hours, or until the salmon is thoroughly cooked.

Lift the salmon out of the slow cooker and transfer to a warmed platter. Remove the foil, snip and remove the string. Serve the salmon warm or cold, with the remaining lemon half cut into wedges for squeezing.

248 CALORIES PER SERVING

chunky monkfish curry

SERVES: 4
PREP: 15 MINUTES
HIGH 3-4 HOURS,
PLUS 1 HOUR
LOW 4-6 HOURS,
PLUS 1 HOUR ON HIGH

1 medium onion
20g chunk of fresh root ginger
2 garlic cloves
1 long green chilli (deseeded first if you like)
20g bunch of fresh coriander, plus extra to garnish
1 tbsp oil
2 tbsp korma or any mild Indian curry paste (from a jar)
227g can chopped tomatoes
50g desiccated coconut
1 tsp flaked sea salt
1 tsp caster sugar
250ml cold water
1 red and 1 green pepper
500g fresh skinless monkfish fillet

Tip: If using thick cod or haddock fillet instead of monkfish, cook the peppers in the sauce for 30 minutes, then add the fish, cover and cook for a further 15-20 minutes.

This is a deliciously light Goan-style fish curry that uses desiccated coconut instead of coconut milk. The long, slow cooking tenderises the firm monkfish and softens and brings out the coconut flavour. You can swap monkfish for fillets of another firm fish but reduce the cooking times as I've suggested below.

Peel and thinly slice the onion, peel and finely grate the ginger and peel and crush the garlic. Thinly slice the green chilli, and finely chop the coriander, including the stalks.

Heat the oil in a large non-stick frying pan and fry the onion over a medium heat for 3-5 minutes, stirring frequently until softened and lightly browned. Add the garlic and ginger and cook for a further minute, stirring. Stir the curry paste into the pan and fry for a few seconds, stirring continuously.

Tip the spiced onions into the slow cooker and stir in the chopped tomatoes, chilli, coriander, coconut, salt, sugar and water. Cover with the lid and cook on HIGH for 3-4 hours or LOW for 4-6 hours, or until the spices have mellowed and the sauce has thickened.

Deseed and cut the peppers into roughly 3cm chunks. Remove the slow cooker lid and stir the peppers into the curry sauce. Cut the fish into roughly 3cm chunky pieces and place on top. Cover again and cook for a further hour on HIGH, or until the fish is tender and thoroughly cooked. Serve with basmati rice.

sweet
things

125
CALORIES
PER SERVING

creamy rice pudding

SERVES 6

PREP: 5 MINUTES

LOW 3-4 HOURS

10g butter, for greasing
100g pudding rice
500ml semi-skimmed milk
25g golden caster sugar

Tip: If you prefer your rice pudding cold, make it with 750ml milk instead. The rice pudding will continue to thicken as it cools.

This creamy-tasting rice pudding is a doddle to make. It can be served topped with my fruity low-sugar strawberry jam, and because the jam is thickened with cornflour rather than sugar, you need a lot less.

Grease the inside of your slow cooker pot with butter. Add the rice, milk and sugar, stir gently, then cover with the lid and cook on LOW for 3-4 hours, or until the rice is tender and creamy. Spoon into six dessert dishes and top with fresh fruit or low-sugar jam (see recipe below).

Low-sugar strawberry jam: Put 250g hulled and quartered strawberries in a non-stick saucepan with 25g golden caster sugar and 2 tablespoons of cold water. Heat gently, stirring until the sugar dissolves, then bring to a simmer and cook for 5 minutes or until the strawberries are softened and juicy, stirring occasionally.

Mix 2 teaspoons of cornflour with 1 tablespoon of cold water and stir the mixture into the jam. Cook for a further minute until thickened, stirring continuously, then remove from the heat and leave to cool for 10 minutes. Stir the cooled jam and pour into a small, clean pot. Keep covered in the fridge and eat within 3 days. Serves 6. Calories per serving: 32

121
CALORIES
PER SERVING

glam porridge

SERVES 4

PREP: 5 MINUTES

HIGH 1½–2 HOURS

75g jumbo porridge oats
450ml chilled
  semi-skimmed milk
250ml cold water

For a filling breakfast, choose these slow-cooked porridge oats. The long, slow cook makes them taste extra creamy and I've given a couple of fruity variations that really benefit from unhurried cooking.

Put the porridge oats, milk and water in the slow cooker and stir well. Cover with the lid and cook on HIGH for 1½–2 hours. If you get a chance, stir the porridge after it has been cooking for an hour, quickly replacing the lid.

Remove the slow cooker lid and check the oats are tender and very creamy. Spoon the porridge into bowls and serve.

Sour cherry and cinnamon: Add 50g dried sour cherries (or a mixture of dried cherries and cranberries) and a pinch of cinnamon to the oats, milk and water before cooking, and stir well. Cook as above on HIGH then divide between 4 bowls. Top with 4 tablespoons of half-fat crème fraiche and sprinkle with 15g grated plain dark chocolate. Serves 4. Calories per serving with porridge: 190

Tropical fruit: Add 50g mixed dried pineapple, mango and papaya chunks and 15g desiccated coconut to the oats, milk and water before cooking, and stir well. Cook as above on HIGH then divide between 4 bowls and top with 2 small sliced bananas, 10g toasted flaked coconut (coconut chips) and 4 heaped tablespoons of full-fat natural yoghurt. Serves 4. Calories per serving with porridge: 259

34
CALORIES
PER SERVING

poached rhubarb
with vanilla

SERVES 4

PREP: 5 MINUTES

HIGH 45 MINUTES–1 HOUR

25g caster sugar
100ml cold water
1 vanilla pod or ½ tsp vanilla
 bean paste
400g young, slender
 rhubarb
half-fat crème fraiche, single
 cream or natural yoghurt,
 to serve

Fabulous for breakfast or as a light summer pudding, poached rhubarb is a real treat. Raw rhubarb also freezes surprisingly well, so take advantage of it while it is in season and cut it into short lengths before freezing.

Put the sugar in a small bowl and stir in the water. Cut the vanilla pod in half lengthways and scrape the seeds out of one half with the point of a knife. Add the seeds to the water.

Stir together until the seeds are dispersed as evenly as possible through the water. Don't worry if they cluster into small lumps. Wrap the remaining half pod tightly in cling film and try to use within 1 month as it will harden over time. Alternatively, stir the vanilla paste into the water and sugar.

Trim the rhubarb and cut it into roughly 6–8cm lengths. Put the rhubarb and the vanilla and water mixture into the slow cooker and stir together. Cover with the lid and cook on HIGH for 45 minutes to 1 hour, or until the rhubarb is just tender but still holding its shape (the time will depend on the thickness of the rhubarb stems).

Adjust the sweetness to taste – trying to keep sugar to an absolute minimum. Serve warm or cold with half-fat crème fraiche, single cream or natural yoghurt.

243

CALORIES
PER SERVING

no-fuss crème caramel

SERVES 4
**PREP: 15 MINUTES,
PLUS COOLING**
LOW 2–2½ HOURS

oil, for greasing
100g caster sugar
3 tbsp cold water
2 large eggs, plus 2 large
    egg yolks
1½ tsp vanilla extract
300ml semi-skimmed milk

Tip: It's best if the dishes fit
in a single layer in the slow
cooker, but don't worry too
much if one or two of the
dishes have to sit on top of
the others – just make sure
they are nicely spread out
and only add enough water
to reach halfway up the
sides of the dishes on the
bottom layer.

My family adore crème caramel, but I'd always found it a bit
of a fiddle to make. No longer! The slow cooker helps create
the most perfect lower-calorie custards without the worry
of overbaking. Give it a go – you will be amazed.

Lightly grease the insides of four 175ml metal mini pudding tins
(dariole moulds) or ramekins with oil, and set aside.

Put half the sugar in a small saucepan and add the cold water.
Stir well and place over a medium-high heat. Bring to a simmer
and cook for 4–6 minutes, without stirring, or until the sugar
dissolves and the caramel turns a deep chestnut brown. Swirl
the caramel gently in the pan as it cooks, but take care to avoid
splashes. (Do not be tempted to touch or taste the caramel as it
will be extremely hot.)

Divide the caramel between the four greased dishes, so it
lightly coats the base of each one. (Take care, as the hot
caramel will heat the bottom of the tins quickly.) Leave to
stand for 30 minutes, to allow the caramel to harden.

Whisk the eggs and egg yolks together with the remaining
sugar and the vanilla extract with a large metal whisk until well
combined but not frothy. Stir in the milk and strain into a large
jug.

Divide the custard mixture equally between each of the dishes
and cover the top of each one tightly with foil, pinching around
the edges to seal. Place in the slow cooker and pour in enough
cold water to come halfway up the sides of each dish. Cover
with the lid and cook on LOW for 2–2½ hours, or until set.

Remove the crème caramels from the slow cooker, holding the
dishes with an oven glove. Leave to cool for 30 minutes, then
transfer to the fridge for several hours or overnight.

To serve, remove the foil lids and press the surface of each
pudding gently with your finger or a teaspoon to break the seal
all around the edge. Invert on to small plates and give a couple
of little shakes until the puddings flop down on to the dishes.

229
CALORIES
PER SERVING

apple syrup sponge pudding

SERVES 6

PREP: 15 MINUTES

HIGH 2-3 HOURS

50g softened butter,
   plus extra for greasing
50g soft light brown sugar
2 large eggs
125g self-raising flour
50ml semi-skimmed milk
finely grated zest of 1 lemon
2 eating apples
   (about 140g each)
1 tbsp golden syrup
half-fat crème fraiche,
   to serve (optional)

No slow cooker book would be complete without a proper steamed pudding – and this is my version. It's packed with apples to reduce the overall calories, and the syrup is poured on afterwards so you need less of it. Any leftovers are really nice served cold with a cuppa, too.

Lightly butter an 800ml heat-proof pudding basin, and line the base with a small disc of baking parchment. (The basin should have a diameter of around 15cm at the top.) Beat the butter, sugar, eggs and flour together in a large mixing bowl using an electric whisk until thick and smooth. Beat in the milk and lemon zest.

Peel the apples and cut into quarters. Remove the cores and cut the apples into roughly 2cm chunks. Stir the apples into the pudding batter then spoon into the prepared basin. Cover the top of the basin with a piece of foil, and pinch tightly around the edges to seal.

Place in the slow cooker and add enough just-boiled water to come halfway up the sides of the pudding. Cover with the lid and cook on HIGH for 2–3 hours or until well risen and cooked throughout.

Carefully take the basin out of the slow cooker. Holding it with a dry tea towel in one hand, loosen the sides of the sponge very carefully with a round-ended knife and turn out very gently on to a warmed plate. Remove the baking parchment and drizzle over the syrup. Serve immediately, with half-fat crème fraiche if you like.

211
CALORIES
PER SERVING

maple and pecan baked apples

SERVES 4
PREP: 10 MINUTES
HIGH 1½–2 HOURS
LOW 4–6 HOURS

40g pecan nuts
100g mixed dried fruit
    (raisins, sultanas, currants
    and peel)
½ tsp ground cinnamon
1 lemon
4 medium Bramley cooking
    apples (about 250g each)
1 tbsp maple syrup or clear
    honey
75ml cold water
fromage frais or half-fat
    crème fraiche, to serve

A simple, throw-together recipe and classic low-calorie dessert. I like to use mixed dried fruit containing raisins, sultanas, currants and peel, but you could simply use sultanas or raisins if you have them handy. Serve warm for pudding or cold as a fruity breakfast topped with a handful of fresh blueberries and natural yoghurt.

Break the pecan nuts into small pieces with your fingers and put them in a bowl. Add the dried fruit and cinnamon then finely grate the lemon zest and add it to the bowl. Toss together. Squeeze the lemon juice.

Cut the top quarter off each apple on a board. Then, using a small spoon (a 5ml teaspoon works well), melon baller or knife, carefully remove the core without going right through the base. Place the larger apple pieces cut side up in the slow cooker.

Fill with the mixed fruit and nuts (don't worry if some sits on top of the apples too) and drizzle with the maple syrup or honey then replace the cut apple 'lids'. Pour the lemon juice and water over the apples, cover with the lid and cook on HIGH for 1½–2 hours or LOW for 4–6 hours, or until softened. Serve with fromage frais or half-fat crème fraiche.

179

light farmhouse cake

SERVES 16
PREP: 25 MINUTES
HIGH 2–2½ HOURS

100g butter, well softened,
plus extra for greasing
200g ready-to-eat prunes
1 medium orange
200g mixed dried fruit
75g soft light brown sugar
2 tsp mixed spice
3 large eggs
1 tsp baking powder
200g plain flour

Freeze all or part of the
cooked and cooled cake
tightly wrapped in foil and
placed in a large labelled
freezer bag for up to 2
months. Unwrap and thaw
at room temperature for 3–5
hours before serving.

Who would have thought you could cook a cake in a slow
cooker? But you can. This light fruit cake is fantastically moist,
far lower in sugar than a traditional fruit cake and isn't too rich
and heavy. It's best to use a round slow cooker, but an oval pot
will still work really well – you'll just end up with a slightly
strangely shaped cake once baked.

Lightly grease the base and sides of a roughly 4.5-litre capacity
slow cooker with butter then line the base with a double layer
of baking parchment. The best way to do this is to draw around
the base of the slow cooker with a pencil on a folded piece of
baking parchment and cut out the shape.

Cut long strips of baking parchment to go around the sides.
If you snip 2cm into the strips every 3cm, it should fit around the
slow cooker pot more snugly and the butter will help it stick.

Cut the prunes into quarters. Finely grate the zest of the orange
then cut the orange in half and squeeze the juice. Put the
orange zest and juice, prunes, mixed dried fruit, sugar and
mixed spice into a large non-stick saucepan. Add the butter
and place the pan over a gentle heat. Cook for 4–5 minutes, or
until the butter melts, stirring continuously. Remove from the
heat and leave to cool for 10 minutes.

Beat the eggs until well combined and stir into the dried fruit.
Add the baking powder and flour and stir well together until
thick and creamy. Spoon the cake batter into the prepared slow
cooker and level the surface with the back of a spoon.

Cover loosely with a piece of baking parchment then pop the
lid on top and cook on HIGH for 2–2½ hours or until the cake is
cooked and a skewer inserted into the centre of the cake comes
out clean. It won't have the crunchy top of an oven-baked cake
but should be beginning to brown around the sides. Remove
the pot from the slow cooker and leave the cake to cool in the
pot for 30 minutes. Carefully turn it out, peel off the lining
paper and leave to cool completely.

346
CALORIES
PER SERVING

squidgy chocolate puddings

SERVES 6

PREP: 20 MINUTES

HIGH 2-3 HOURS

75g softened butter,
   plus extra for greasing
50g dry white breadcrumbs
   or panko breadcrumbs
200ml semi-skimmed milk
3 medium eggs
75g golden caster sugar
100g self-raising flour
25g cocoa powder
6 squares of plain dark
   chocolate (around 50g)
½ tsp each cocoa powder
   and icing sugar, mixed,
   to decorate

Freeze the cooled and
cooked puddings out of
their tins and wrapped
tightly in foil for up to
1 month. Unwrap and thaw
at room temperature for
1-2 hours then reheat on
individual heat-proof plates,
covered with a microwave-
proof bowl, for about
1 minute on HIGH, or until
hot throughout.

These chocolate puddings are made using breadcrumbs, which helps reduce the calories, and they each contain a secret square of dark chocolate that melts as they cook. They reheat well in the microwave, so it's worth making the full batch even if you aren't serving six people.

Lightly grease six 175–200ml metal pudding basins (dariole moulds) with butter and line the bases with small discs of baking parchment. Put the breadcrumbs in a bowl and stir in the milk. Leave to stand for 10 minutes.

While the breadcrumbs are soaking, place the butter, eggs, sugar, and flour in a large mixing bowl. Sift in the cocoa powder and beat together using an electric whisk until light and fluffy. Add the breadcrumbs and milk and continue whisking for a few seconds more until thick and creamy.

Spoon the cake batter into the prepared basins. Push a square of chocolate into the centre of each pudding then smooth the surface. Cover the top of each pudding with a piece of foil, and pinch along the edges to seal.

Place the puddings in the slow cooker, in two layers if necessary, and add enough just-boiled water from a kettle to come halfway up the sides of the puddings on the bottom layer. Cover with the lid and cook on HIGH for 2–3 hours, or until well risen and fully cooked.

Remove the lid, take the puddings out of the slow cooker and remove the foil. Holding each pudding with a folded, dry tea towel in one hand, loosen the sides of the chocolate sponges very carefully with a round-ended knife and turn out gently on to six plates. Remove the baking parchment and dust the puddings with sifted icing sugar mixed with a little cocoa. Serve immediately.

159
CALORIES
PER SERVING

st clement's cake

SERVES 16

PREP: 25 MINUTES

LOW 6-8 HOURS,
PLUS HIGH 2-2½ HOURS

2 small oranges, washed
   (about 150g each)
1 lemon, washed (about
   110g)
350ml cold water
oil, for greasing
200g ground almonds
5 large eggs
50g self-raising flour
100g golden caster sugar

FOR THE LEMON SYRUP
1 lemon
3 tbsp cold water
25g golden caster sugar

Freeze all or part of the
cooked and cooled cake
tightly wrapped in foil and
placed in a large labelled
freezer bag for up to 2
months. Unwrap and thaw
at room temperature for
3-4 hours before serving.

Tip: If you don't have a
round slow cooker the right
size, bake in the tin at
180°C/Fan 160°C/Gas 4 for
40-50 minutes instead.

Check the manufacturer's
instructions to make sure
that your slow cooker is
suitable for cooking without
added liquid.

Whole fruit is softened in the slow cooker before being transformed into a naturally sweet purée as the base for this deliciously moist cake. If you don't have a round slow cooker, you can cook the fruit in any size slow cooker, then finish the cake in the oven.

Place the whole oranges and lemon in your slow cooker. Add the cold water, cover with the lid and cook on LOW for 6-8 hours or until the fruit is completely soft. Turn off and leave to cool.

Lightly grease a 18cm spring clip cake tin with oil and line the base and sides with baking parchment. Take the fruit out of the slow cooker. Cut the orange and lemon into quarters and flick out any pips. Place the fruit in a food processor and blitz to a purée. Add the ground almonds, eggs, flour and sugar. Blitz on the pulse setting until the ingredients form a thick batter.

Pour the cake batter into the prepared tin, place in the slow cooker and cover with the lid. Cook on HIGH for 2-2½ hours, or until a skewer inserted into the centre of the cake comes out moist but clean.

Carefully remove the cake from the slow cooker and allow to cool slightly. To make the lemon syrup, thinly pare the lemon zest and squeeze the juice. Put the zest and all the juice in a small saucepan with the water and sugar. Bring to the boil and cook for 4-6 minutes, or until reduced and syrupy.

Take the cake out of the tin, peel off the lining paper and place on a wire rack. Drizzle with the lemon syrup while it's still warm. Cut into slender slices and serve with fresh fruit and half-fat crème fraîche or natural bio yoghurt. Store in a sealed container in the fridge for up to 3 days.

99
CALORIES
PER SERVING

plum and apple crunch

SERVES 6
PREP: 10 MINUTES
HIGH 2–3 HOURS
LOW 4–6 HOURS

750g fresh plums
3 eating apples
50g golden caster sugar
1 tsp mixed spice
1 star anise
75ml cold water

Tip: If any of the plum stones are too hard to remove, simply cook with them attached and scoop them out once the fruit is cooked.

Check the manufacturer's instructions to make sure that your slow cooker is suitable for cooking without added liquid.

Enjoy this poached fruit compote for breakfast with spoonfuls of natural yoghurt or as a pudding with half-fat crème fraiche or custard. Warm or cold, it is utterly delicious and will keep well in the fridge for up to three days, so you don't need to eat it all at once. The crunchy oat topping has a lovely texture without the heaviness of a traditional crumble.

Cut the plums in half, remove the stones and place the plums in the slow cooker. Peel the apples, cut them into quarters, remove the cores then thickly slice. Add the apples to the slow cooker and stir in the sugar, spices and water. Cover with the lid and cook on HIGH for 2–3 hours or LOW for 4–6 hours, or until the fruit is softened but still holding its shape.

Serve warm, or leave to cool. Sprinkle with a little maple crunch (see below) and add spoonfuls of natural yoghurt, half-fat crème fraiche or single cream. (Don't eat the star anise – discard it when you serve.)

Maple crunch: Put 25g butter and 150g jumbo porridge oats in the slow cooker. Cook on HIGH for about 1½ hours, without a lid and stirring every 20–30 minutes, or until the oats are beginning to turn golden. Stir in 1 tablespoon of maple syrup and cook for a further 15 minutes, stirring every 5 minutes. Leave to cool in the pot. Keep in an airtight jar and use within 2 weeks. (You can also cook the maple crunch in a dry frying pan over a low heat, reducing the cooking time.) Serves 6. Calories per serving: 129

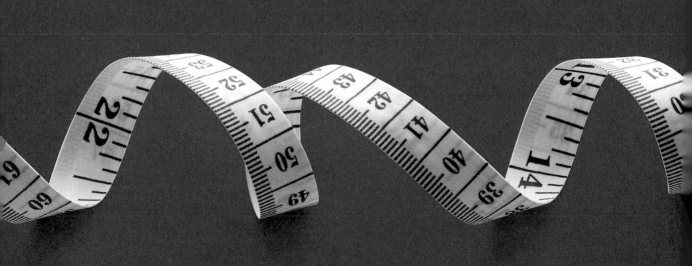

other
things

139
CALORIES
PER SERVING

mixed root soup

SERVES 6
PREP: 20 MINUTES
HIGH 4–5 HOURS
LOW 8–10 HOURS

2 medium onions
2 garlic cloves
1 tbsp oil
500g carrots (about
    5 medium)
300g sweet potato
    (about 1 large)
250g parsnip (about 1 large)
1.25 litres hot vegetable
    stock (made with 1
    vegetable stock cube)
flaked sea salt
ground black pepper

Flat-freeze the cooked
and cooled soup in labelled
zip-seal bags for up to
3 months. Place the frozen
soup into a large non-stick
saucepan, add a splash of
water and reheat, stirring
frequently, until piping hot.
Alternatively, thaw in the
fridge overnight and reheat
in a saucepan or the
microwave.

Tip: Frying the onion first
adds a good depth of
flavour to the soup, so try
not to miss this step out if
you have time.

I'm a huge fan of making root vegetable soups in the slow
cooker. It's a great way of using up the vegetables that tend
to lurk at the bottom of the fridge, and it is almost foolproof.
You can use roughly 1kg of any root vegetables for this recipe
and it will work just as well.

Peel and thinly slice the onions and peel and crush the garlic.
Heat the oil in a large non-stick saucepan and gently fry the
onions for 10 minutes, or until softened and lightly browned,
stirring occasionally. Add the garlic and cook for a further
minute, stirring. While the onion is cooking, peel the carrots,
sweet potato and parsnip and cut into roughly 3cm chunks.

Transfer the onion and garlic to the slow cooker and add the
other vegetables and the stock. Season with a little salt and
plenty of pepper. Cover with the lid and cook on HIGH for
4–5 hours or LOW for 8–10 hours, or until the vegetables are
very soft.

Carefully take the pot out of the slow-cooker base and remove
the lid. Leave the soup to cool for a few minutes. Transfer to a
food processor and blitz until as smooth as possible (you may
need to do this in two or three batches). Alternatively, blitz with
a stick blender until smooth. Transfer to a saucepan and reheat
gently just before serving, stirring continuously and adding
extra water or a splash of semi-skimmed milk if necessary.
Adjust the seasoning to taste and ladle into bowls to serve.

72
CALORIES
PER SERVING

celeriac soup

SERVES 6
PREP: 20 MINUTES
HIGH 3½–4½ HOURS
LOW 7–9 HOURS

2 medium onions
2 garlic cloves
1 tbsp oil
1 large celeriac (about 825g)
1 litre hot vegetable stock
   (made with 1 vegetable
   stock cube)
100ml semi-skimmed milk
flaked sea salt
ground black pepper

Flat-freeze the cooked
and cooled soup in labelled
zip-seal bags for up to
3 months. Place the frozen
soup in a wide-based non-
stick saucepan, add a splash
of water and reheat, stirring
frequently, until piping hot.
Alternatively, thaw in the
fridge overnight and reheat
in a saucepan or the
microwave.

Tip: Top the soup with
crunchy baked bread
croutons and mixed seeds,
adding 45 calories for every
10g of croutons and 30
calories for every teaspoon
of mixed seeds. For home-
made croutons, cut bread
into small cubes and spritz
with a little oil. Place on a
baking tray and cook in a
preheated oven at 200°C/
Fan 180°C/Gas 6 for 10–15
minutes, turning once.

I used to make celeriac soup on a weekly basis through winter
during my first cooking job, and I never tired of it. The slow
cooker is perfect for drawing out the sweet, mellow flavour
of celeriac and it can be left for hours without spoiling. Top
with mixed seeds or croutons to contrast with the velvety
texture of the soup, if you like.

Peel and thinly slice the onions and peel and crush the garlic.
Heat the oil in a large non-stick saucepan and gently fry the
onions for 10 minutes, or until softened and lightly browned,
stirring occasionally. Add the garlic and cook for a further
minute, stirring. While the onion is cooking, peel the celeriac
and cut into roughly 3cm chunks.

Transfer the onion and garlic to the slow cooker and add the
celeriac and stock. Season with a little salt and plenty of
pepper. Cover with the lid and cook on HIGH for 3½–4½ hours
or LOW for 7–9 hours, or until the celeriac is very soft.

Carefully take the pot out of the slow-cooker base and remove
the lid. Leave the soup to cool for a few minutes. Transfer to a
food processor and blitz until as smooth as possible (you may
need to do this in 2 or 3 batches). Alternatively, blitz with a stick
blender until smooth. Transfer to a saucepan and add the milk.
Reheat gently just before serving, stirring continuously. Adjust
the seasoning to taste and ladle into bowls. Top with croutons
and mixed seeds, if you like.

76
CALORIES
PER SERVING

french-style yoghurt

SERVES 6

**PREP: 5 MINUTES,
PLUS COOLING**

LOW 30 MINUTES

600ml full-fat milk
75g plain natural live
    yoghurt (not low-fat)

Tip: Ceramic cooker pots
work best for making
yoghurt as they retain heat
much better. If using a metal
slow cooker pot, you will
need to remove it from the
slow cooker base after the
cooking time and cover the
closed pot with a thick, dry
towel to help retain the
heat, otherwise the yoghurt
may not set thickly enough.

These little lightly-set yoghurts are mild and naturally sweet.
They are very easy to make and can be stored in the fridge
for up to 3 days. Top with fresh berries for a delicious and
healthy breakfast, or serve as a simple snack any time. Use
small heat-proof glass pots or ramekins which hold between
125 and 150ml.

Pour the milk into a large saucepan and bring to boiling point,
stirring occasionally. Watch the milk carefully because it could
boil over – using a big pan makes this less likely. As soon as the
milk begins to boil, reduce the heat so the temperature drops
quickly.

Simmer the milk very gently for 2 minutes, stirring occasionally
with a wooden spoon. Remove from the heat, pour into a large
heat-proof measuring jug and leave to cool for 30 minutes. Stir
every now and then so a skin doesn't form.

Whisk the yoghurt into the milk and pour the mixture into six
125ml ramekins or heat-proof glass pots. Cover each one with
foil and press around the edge to seal. (This will prevent water
dripping on to the yoghurts as they cook.)

Place in the slow cooker, ideally in one layer. Add about 500ml
cold water (it shouldn't rise more than halfway up the bottom
layer of the pots) and cover with the lid. Cook on LOW for
30 minutes then turn off the slow cooker and leave to stand
for 6–8 hours before transferring to the fridge. Keep chilled and
eat within 3 days.

186

jacket potatoes

SERVES 4

PREP: 5 MINUTES

HIGH 4–5 HOURS

4 medium-large potatoes
(each about 230g, ideally
Maris Piper)
2 tsp oil
flaked sea salt
ground black pepper

Tip: Check the
manufacturer's instructions
to make sure that your slow
cooker is suitable for
cooking without added
liquid.

Slow-cooked potatoes are perfect for a no-hassle lunch. Pop
them on in the morning and by lunchtime you will have a light,
fluffy potato without having to use the oven. A medium-large
potato contains about 186 calories and can be filled with a
variety of lower calorie ingredients, to make a healthy and
satisfying meal. I've given the method for four potatoes but
it will work just as well with two or six spuds.

Loosely line the slow cooker with a piece of baking parchment
that covers the bottom and comes about 5cm up the sides. This
will help trap the water from the steam as it drips down the
sides of the slow cooker, and should prevent the potatoes
becoming soggy.

Pierce the potatoes a couple of times with a fork and rub with
the oil. Season with salt and pepper. Scrunch up four small
pieces of foil into conker-sized pieces and place them on top of
the baking parchment, spaced evenly apart.

Place the potatoes on top of the foil mounds. Cooking them
on top of the foil will prevent the potatoes becoming hard
underneath. Cover with the lid and cook on HIGH for 4–5 hours,
or until soft throughout.

379

loaded sweet potatoes

4 medium sweet potatoes
    (each around 300g)
150g long-stemmed
    broccoli
oil, for spraying or brushing
2 rashers rindless back
    bacon
4 tbsp soured cream or
    half-fat crème fraiche
40g mature Cheddar
    cheese
flaked sea salt
ground black pepper

Tip: If your potatoes don't
fit in one layer, place them
on top of each other
instead.

Check the manufacturer's
instructions to make sure
that your slow cooker is
suitable for cooking without
added liquid.

Cooking potatoes in a slow cooker means you don't have to heat your oven for hours. I've suggested a delicious filling of long-stemmed broccoli, bacon and cheese for these sweet potatoes, but they are just as good served simply as a main meal accompaniment, perhaps with pan-fried chicken or fish and a large mixed salad.

Loosely line the slow cooker with a piece of baking parchment that covers the bottom and comes about 5cm up the sides. This will help trap the water from the steam as it drips down the sides of the slow cooker and should prevent the potatoes becoming soggy. Pierce the potatoes a couple of times with a fork. Scrunch up four small pieces of foil into conker-sized pieces and place them on top of the baking parchment, spaced evenly apart.

Place the potatoes on top of the foil mounds. Cooking them on top of the foil will prevent the potatoes becoming hard underneath. Cover with the lid and cook on HIGH for 3½–4½ hours, or until soft throughout.

When the potatoes are ready, pour enough water into a saucepan to fill it one-third full, and bring to the boil. Trim the broccoli and add it to the bubbling water, return to the boil and cook for 2–3 minutes, or until tender. Drain in a colander.

While the broccoli is cooking, brush or spray a non-stick frying pan with a little oil and place over a medium-high heat. Add the bacon and cook for 2–3 minutes, or until nicely browned and crisp in places. Tip on to a board and cut into small pieces.

Transfer the potatoes to a baking tray or grill pan and split open with a knife. Top with the hot broccoli, soured cream or crème fraiche and chopped bacon. Coarsely grate the cheese and sprinkle on top. Place under a preheated hot grill for 1–2 minutes, or until the cheese melts. Season with pepper and serve immediately, with a large mixed salad, if you like.

99
CALORIES
PER SERVING

basic korma sauce

SERVES 12
PREP: 25 MINUTES
HIGH 3–4 HOURS
LOW 7–9 HOURS

6 large onions
1 tbsp oil
6 garlic cloves
75g chunk of fresh root
    ginger
125g korma curry paste
    (or any mild Indian curry
    paste, from a jar)
1 tbsp caster sugar
2 tsp flaked sea salt, plus
    extra to season
600ml just-boiled water
3 tbsp double cream
ground black pepper

Flat-freeze the cooked
and cooled sauce in labelled
zip-seal bags for up to
3 months. Place the frozen
sauce in a non-stick
saucepan, add 100ml water
for each 350ml sauce and
reheat, stirring frequently,
until piping hot.

Tip: 350ml will make
enough for a curry for
4 people. Add an extra
100ml of water for each
350ml of sauce when you
reheat it. It will keep well in
the fridge, covered, for up
to 3 days.

With the help of your slow cooker it's easy to make a delicious home-made korma sauce in bulk and then freeze it in portions so it's always to hand. All you then need to add is some fresh chicken, prawns or fish for brilliant curry in a hurry. Don't be put off by the thought of chopping all those onions – I promise it's worth it!

Peel and roughly chop the onions. Heat the oil in a wide-based non-stick saucepan and fry the onions over a medium-high heat for 15 minutes, or until softened and nicely browned, stirring regularly. While the onions are cooking, peel and crush the garlic and peel and finely grate the ginger. Stir the garlic, ginger and curry paste into the onions and cook for a further 3 minutes, stirring continuously. Don't let the garlic burn. Tip the spiced onions into the slow cooker.

Add the sugar, salt and water to the slow cooker and stir well. Cover with the lid and cook on HIGH for 3–4 hours or LOW for 7–9 hours, or until the sauce looks thick and rich. Carefully take the pot out of the slow-cooker and remove the lid. Leave to cool for a few minutes. Transfer to a food processor and blitz until smooth. Stir in the cream and adjust the seasoning.

Chicken korma: Cut 4 x 150g skinless chicken breasts into roughly 3cm chunks. Heat 1 tablespoon of oil in a large non-stick frying pan or wok and stir-fry the chicken for 5 minutes. Add 350ml of cooked korma sauce and 100ml cold water and bring to a gentle simmer. Cook for a further 4–5 minutes, or until the chicken is thoroughly cooked, stirring frequently. Top with 1 tablespoon of double or single cream, 15g toasted flaked almonds and some fresh coriander. Serves 4. Calories per serving: 325

Prawn korma: Put 350ml of cooked korma sauce and 100ml cold water into a large non-stick frying pan or wok and bring to a gentle simmer, stirring. Add 350g peeled raw tiger prawns and cook for a further 2–3 minutes, or until the prawns are thoroughly cooked, stirring frequently. Serves 4. Calories per serving: 171

109

basic balti sauce

SERVES 12
PREP: 25 MINUTES
HIGH 3–4 HOURS
LOW 7–9 HOURS

6 large onions
2 tbsp oil
6 garlic cloves
50g chunk of fresh root
  ginger
50g bunch of fresh
  coriander
150g medium Indian curry
  paste (from a jar)
1 tbsp caster sugar
2 tsp flaked sea salt, plus
  extra to season
2 x 400g cans chopped
  tomatoes
200ml cold water
ground black pepper

Flat-freeze the cooked and
cooled sauce in labelled
zip-seal bags for up to
3 months. Place the frozen
sauce into a large, non-stick
saucepan, add 150ml water
for each 350ml sauce and
reheat, stirring frequently,
until piping hot.

Indian-style curry paste is widely available and means you can
make a really good home-made curry. Once it's cooked, divide
into smaller portions and freeze.

Peel and roughly chop the onions. Heat the oil in a large
saucepan and fry the onions over a medium-high heat for 15
minutes, or until nicely browned, stirring regularly. While the
onions are cooking, peel and crush the garlic and peel and
finely grate the ginger. Roughly chop the coriander, including
the stalks. Stir the garlic, ginger and curry paste into the onions
and cook for a further 3 minutes, stirring continuously. Don't let
the garlic burn. Tip the spiced onions into the slow cooker.

Add the coriander, sugar, salt, canned tomatoes and water to
the onions, season with plenty of pepper and stir well. Cover
with the lid and cook on HIGH for 3–4 hours or LOW for 7–9
hours, or until the sauce looks thick and rich, and the spices
have mellowed.

Carefully take the pot out of the slow-cooker base and remove
the lid. Either keep the sauce chunky or leave it to cool for a few
minutes then transfer to a food processor and blend until as
smooth as possible (perhaps in batches). Alternatively, blitz
with a stick blender until smooth. Adjust the seasoning.

Use the sauce immediately or leave it to cool completely.
Transfer to a large jug and divide into suitable portions – 350ml
will make enough curry for 4 people. Add an extra 100ml of
water for each 350ml of sauce when you reheat it. It will keep
well in the fridge, covered, for up to 3 days.

Balti chicken: Cut 4 x 150g skinless chicken breasts into
roughly 3cm chunks. Deseed a red and a yellow pepper and cut
into roughly 3cm chunks. Heat 1 tablespoon of oil in a large
non-stick frying pan or wok and stir-fry the chicken and
peppers over a medium-high heat for 5 minutes. Add 350ml of
cooked balti sauce and 150ml cold water and bring to a gentle
simmer. Cook for a further 4–5 minutes, or until the chicken is
thoroughly cooked, stirring frequently. Serves 4. Calories per
serving: 315

270

basic bolognese

SERVES 8
PREP: 15 MINUTES
HIGH 4–5 HOURS
LOW 6–8 HOURS

800g lean minced beef
(10% fat or less)
2 medium onions
4 garlic cloves
300g closed-cup or button
mushrooms
100g dried red split lentils
100ml just-boiled water
2 beef stock cubes
1 tbsp Marmite
3 tbsp tomato purée (50g)
2 x 400g cans chopped
tomatoes
150ml red wine
2 tsp dried oregano or dried
mixed herbs
1 fresh bay leaf or 2 dried
bay leaves
ground black pepper

Flat-freeze the cooked
and cooled Bolognese in
labelled zip-seal bags for
up to 3 months. Place the
frozen sauce in a large, non-
stick saucepan. Add a
splash of water and reheat
over a medium heat, stirring
gently, until piping hot.
Alternatively, thaw
overnight in the fridge
before reheating.

A basic Bolognese sauce can be used for spaghetti Bolognese,
lasagne or pasta bakes, as a filling for jacket potatoes or as a
base for a cottage pie. You can make it in bulk in the slow
cooker and then freeze it in convenient portions, so there
is no excuse for not eating healthily.

Put the mince in a large wide-based saucepan over a medium
heat and fry for 6–8 minutes, stirring and squishing against the
side of the pan with two wooden spoons to break up the beef.
Peel and finely chop the onion, and crush the garlic. Thickly
slice the mushrooms (halve the button mushrooms or leave
whole if small).

Transfer the mince to your slow cooker and add the onions,
garlic and mushrooms. Rinse the lentils in a sieve under cold
running water and stir into the pot.

Pour the just-boiled water into a heat-proof jug, add the stock
cubes and Marmite and stir until dissolved. Add the tomato
purée and mix well. This will help add flavour to the Bolognese.
Stir the stock mixture into the beef mixture and add the canned
tomatoes and red wine, herbs and plenty of pepper.

Cover with the lid and cook on HIGH for 4–5 hours or LOW
for 6–8 hours, or until the beef and vegetables are tender.
Adjust the seasoning to taste. Use the sauce immediately or
leave it to cool completely and freeze in suitable portions (bags
containing two portions of the sauce tend to be the most
convenient).

55
CALORIES
PER SERVING

simple tomato pasta sauce

SERVES 10
PREP: 15 MINUTES
HIGH 3-4 HOURS
LOW 8-10 HOURS

4 medium onions
4 garlic cloves
2 tbsp oil
4 x 400g cans chopped
    tomatoes
1 tbsp dried oregano or
    mixed dried herbs
2 fresh bay leaves or
    3 dried bay leaves
½-1 tsp dried chilli flakes, to
    taste (optional)
1 tsp flaked sea salt
1 tsp caster sugar (optional)
ground black pepper

Flat-freeze the cooked and
cooled sauce in labelled
zip-seal bags for up to
3 months. Place the frozen
sauce in a large non-stick
saucepan, add a splash of
water and reheat, stirring
frequently until piping hot.
Alternatively, thaw
overnight in the fridge
before reheating.

This is a great, basic tomato sauce that can be used as a base
for all kinds of pasta dishes. It makes enough to serve about 10
people, so you can freeze it in handy portions and then reheat
it from frozen – it could save you a fortune in takeaway meals
and trips to the local store.

Peel and finely chop the onions and peel and crush the garlic.
Heat the oil in a large, non-stick saucepan, and fry the onions
over a medium-high heat for 12–15 minutes, or until softened
and nicely browned, stirring frequently. Add the garlic and cook
for a further minute, stirring continuously.

Transfer the onions and garlic to the slow cooker and stir in the
tomatoes, herbs and chilli flakes, if using. Season with the salt
and plenty of pepper. Cover with the lid and cook on HIGH for
3–4 hours or LOW for 8–10 hours, or until the sauce tastes rich
and sweet. Adjust the seasoning to taste, adding a teaspoon of
sugar if necessary.

Use the sauce immediately or leave it to cool completely and
freeze in suitable portions (bags containing two portions of the
sauce tend to be most convenient).

25
CALORIES
PER 100ML

chicken stock

MAKES ABOUT 1.3 LITRES

PREP: 10 MINUTES

LOW 7–9 HOURS

1–2 chicken carcasses
1 medium onion
2 large carrots
2 celery sticks
2 fresh bay leaves or
   3 dried bay leaves
small bunch of fresh thyme
   or 1 tsp dried thyme
1 tsp flaked sea salt
10 black peppercorns
1.5 litres cold water

Freeze the cooked and cooled stock in labelled freezer-proof containers for up to 3 months. Reheat from frozen very gently in a saucepan over a low heat. Once thawed, bring to the boil and cook for 5 minutes.

A good home-made chicken stock makes a brilliant base for all types of noodle broths as well as risottos, soups, sauces and gravies. Use the leftover carcass from a roasted chicken, or a couple of chicken carcasses from the butcher for this recipe. You can freeze bones left over from a Sunday lunch until you have enough to make a decent stock.

Place the chicken carcass(es) in the slow cooker, breaking or chopping it into pieces first to fit, if necessary. Discard any skin or fat as you go. Peel and cut the onion into thin wedges, peel and cut the carrots into chunky pieces, and trim and cut the celery into chunky pieces.

Put the vegetables in the slow cooker with the chicken, tucking them in around the carcass(es). Add the bay leaves, thyme, salt, peppercorns and water. The water shouldn't rise more than 5cm from the top of the slow cooker pot, so be prepared to adjust the amount you use if necessary. Cover with the lid and cook on LOW for 7–9 hours, or until the liquid is gently bubbling and the vegetables are very soft.

Carefully strain the stock, bones and vegetables through a colander into a large heat-proof bowl and leave to cool for 30 minutes. (Discard the bones and cooked vegetables.)

Skim off any fat that has floated to the surface of the stock, then strain through a fine sieve into a large jug. It will keep well in the fridge, covered, for up to 2 days.

Note: It's tricky to work out the calories for a home-made stock, so these calculations are based on a ready-made fresh stock, and will vary by a few calories. Don't worry though; stock is so low in calories that it won't make any difference to your weight-loss plans.

28
CALORIES
PER 100ML

beef bone broth

MAKES ABOUT 1.25 LITRES
PREP: 30 MINUTES
LOW 10-12 HOURS

1.5kg beef bones, trimmed
    of fat
2 medium onions
2 large carrots
4 celery sticks
1 fresh bay leaf or
    2 dried bay leaves
small bunch of fresh thyme
    or 1 tsp dried thyme
1 tsp flaked sea salt
10 black peppercorns
2 litres cold water

Freeze the cooked and
cooled stock in labelled
freezer-proof containers for
up to 3 months. Reheat
from frozen very gently in
a saucepan over a low heat.
Once thawed, bring to the
boil and cook for 5 minutes.

Tip: You can get beef bones
from butchers and the meat
department of some
supermarkets. Make sure
they are in pieces small
enough to fit in your slow
cooker, and avoid anything
fatty as it will make the
stock taste greasy.

**Bone broths seem to be all the rage. The long, slow cooking
extracts every bit of flavour from the bones and makes a rich
stock that's great for nourishing soups and can be used to
make lovely Vietnamese or Thai noodle dishes, or to add to
classic beef stews and gravies.**

Preheat the oven to 220°C/Fan 200°C/Gas 7. Place the beef
bones in a roasting tin and cook for 10 minutes. While the
bones are roasting, peel and cut the onions into thin wedges,
peel and cut the carrots into chunky pieces, trim and cut the
celery into chunky pieces. Take the roasting tin out of the oven
and turn the beef bones. Add the vegetables to the roasting tin
and return to the oven for a further 20 minutes.

Take the roasting tin out of the oven and transfer the bones and
vegetables to a large slow cooker, making sure any fat stays in
the tray as it won't be needed for the stock. Add the bay leaf,
thyme, salt and peppercorns and pour over the water. The
water shouldn't rise more than 5cm from the top of the slow
cooker pot, so be prepared to adjust the amount you use If
necessary. Cover with the lid and cook on LOW for 10–12 hours.

Carefully strain the stock, bones and vegetables through a
colander and then a fine sieve into a large bowl and leave to
cool for 30 minutes. (Discard the bones and cooked
vegetables.) Cover and chill until the liquid turns to a firm jelly.

Scrape off the fat that has floated to the surface of the stock
before using it. The stock will keep well in the fridge, covered,
for up to 2 days. Add extra salt to taste when reheating.

Note: It's tricky to work out the calories for a home-made
stock, so these calculations are based on a ready-made fresh
stock, and will vary by a few calories. Don't worry though; stock
is so low in calories that it won't make any difference to your
weight-loss plans.

a few notes on
the recipes

INGREDIENTS

Where possible, choose free-range chicken, meat and eggs. Eggs used in the recipes are medium unless otherwise stated.

All poultry and meat has been trimmed of as much hard or visible fat as possible, although there may be some marbling within the meat. Boneless, skinless chicken breasts weigh around 150g. Fish has been scaled, gutted and pin-boned, and large prawns are deveined. You'll be able to buy most fish and seafood ready prepared, but ask your fishmonger if not and they will be happy to help.

PREPARATION

Do as much preparation as possible before you start to cook. Discard any damaged bits, and wipe or wash fresh produce before preparation unless it's going to be peeled.

Onions, garlic and shallots are peeled unless otherwise stated, and vegetables are trimmed. Lemons, limes and oranges should be well washed before the zest is grated. Weigh fresh herbs in a bunch, then trim off the stalks before chopping the leaves. I've used medium-sized vegetables unless stated. As a rule of thumb, a medium-sized onion and a potato (such as Maris Piper) each weigh about 150g.

All chopped and sliced meat, poultry, fish and vegetable sizes are approximate. Don't worry if your pieces are a bit larger or smaller than indicated, but try to keep roughly to the size so the cooking times are accurate. Even-sized pieces will cook at the same rate, which is especially important for meat and fish.

I love using fresh herbs in my recipes, but you can substitute frozen herbs in most cases. Dried herbs will give a different, more intense, flavour, so use them sparingly.

The recipes have been tested using sunflower oil, but you can substitute vegetable, groundnut or olive oil. I use dark soy sauce in the test kitchen but it's fine to use light instead – it'll give a milder flavour.

CALORIE COUNTS

Nutritional information does not include the optional serving suggestions. When shopping, you may see calories described as kilocalories on food labels; they are the same thing.

HOW TO FREEZE

Freezing food will save you time and money, and lots of the dishes in this book freeze extremely well. If you don't need all the servings at the same time, freeze the rest for another day. Where there are no instructions for freezing a dish, freezing won't give the best results once reheated.

When freezing food, it's important to cool it rapidly after cooking. Separate what you want to freeze from what you're going to serve and place it in a shallow, freezer-proof container. The shallower the container, the quicker the food will cool (putting it in the freezer while it's still warm will raise the freezer temperature and could affect other foods). Cover loosely, then freeze as soon as it's cool.

If you're freezing a lot of food at once, for example after a bulk cooking session or a big shop, flip on the fast-freeze button at least two hours before adding the new dishes and leave it on for 24 hours afterwards. This will reduce the temperature of your freezer and help ensure that food is frozen as rapidly as possible.

When freezing food, expel as much air as possible by wrapping it tightly in a freezer bag or foil to help prevent icy patches, freezer burn and discolouration, or flavour transfer between dishes. Liquids expand when frozen, so leave a 2–3cm gap at the top of containers.

If you have a small freezer and need to save space, flat-freeze thick soups, sauces and casseroles in strong zip-seal freezer bags. Fill the bag half full, then turn it over and flatten it until it is about 1–2cm thick, pressing out as much air as possible and sealing firmly.

Place delicate foods such as breaded chicken or fish fillets and burgers on a tray lined with baking parchment, and freeze in a single layer until solid before placing in containers or freezer bags. This method is called open freezing and helps stop foods sticking together in a block, so you can grab what you need easily.

Label everything clearly, and add the date so you know when to eat it at its best. I aim to use food from the freezer within about 4 months.

DEFROSTING

For the best results, most foods should be defrosted slowly in the fridge for several hours or overnight. For safety's sake, do not thaw dishes at room temperature.

Flat-frozen foods (see above) will thaw and begin to reheat at almost the same time. Just rinse the bag under hot water and break the mixture into a wide-based pan. Add a dash of water and warm over a low heat until thawed. Increase the heat, adding a little more water if necessary, and simmer until piping hot throughout.

Ensure that any foods that have been frozen are thoroughly cooked or reheated before serving.

HOW TO GET THE BEST RESULTS
Measuring with spoons
Spoon measurements are level unless otherwise stated. Use a set of measuring spoons for the best results; they're endlessly useful, especially if you're watching your sugar, salt or fat intake.

1 tsp (1 teaspoon) = 5ml
1 dsp (1 dessertspoon) = 10ml
1 tbsp (1 tablespoon) = 15ml

A scant measure is just below level and a heaped measure is just above. An Australian tablespoon holds 20ml, so Australian cooks should use 3 level teaspoon measures instead.

CONVERSION CHARTS
Oven temperature guide

	Electricity °C	Electricity °F	Electricity (Fan) °C	Gas Mark
Very cool	110	225	90	¹/₄
	120	250	100	¹/₂
Cool	140	275	120	1
	150	300	130	2
Moderate	160	325	140	3
	170	350	160	4
Moderately hot	190	375	170	5
	200	400	180	6
Hot	220	425	200	7
	230	450	210	8
Very hot	240	475	220	9

Liquid measurements

Metric	Imperial	Australian	US
25ml	1fl oz		
60ml	2fl oz	¹/₄ cup	¹/₄ cup
75ml	3fl oz		
100ml	3¹/₂fl oz		
120ml	4fl oz	¹/₂ cup	¹/₂ cup
150ml	5fl oz		
180ml	6fl oz	³/₄ cup	³/₄ cup
200ml	7fl oz		
250ml	9fl oz	1 cup	1 cup
300ml	10¹/₂fl oz	1¹/₄ cups	1¹/₄ cups
350ml	12¹/₂fl oz	1¹/₂ cups	1¹/₂ cups
400ml	14fl oz	1³/₄ cups	1³/₄ cups
450ml	16fl oz	2 cups	2 cups
600ml	1 pint	2¹/₂ cups	2¹/₂ cups
750ml	1¹/₄ pints	3 cups	3 cups
900ml	1¹/₂ pints	3¹/₂ cups	3¹/₂ cups
1 litre	1³/₄ pints	1 quart or 4 cups	1 quart or 4 cups
1.2 litres	2 pints		
1.4 litres	2¹/₂ pints		
1.5 litres	2³/₄ pints		
1.7 litres	3 pints		
2 litres	3¹/₂ pints		

essential extras

Here's my list of suggested 50–150 calorie foods that you can use to supplement the WTC Plan. All calories listed in this list are approximate; a few wayward calories here and there won't make a difference to your allowance. See page 6 for more information on essential extras and how they fit into the plan. I've also listed some 'free' vegetable ideas, of which you can eat as much as you like! Make sure your plate is half filled with vegetables or salad, or serve them in a large bowl on the side. Eating more greens will help fill you up and provide lots of extra nutrients in your diet. Your skin will look better and the weight should drop off.

50 CALORIES PER SERVING

30g (about 5) ready-to-eat dried apricots
15g (1 tbsp) light mayo
30g (2 tbsp) hummus
40g drained artichoke antipasti in oil
60g whole olives

4 fresh apricots
200g fresh blackberries
200g fresh blackcurrants
100g fresh cherries
2 clementines or satsumas
100g fresh figs
½ grapefruit
85g grapes
2 kiwis
100g fresh mango
200g melon
1 medium nectarine
1 medium orange
1 medium peach
1 medium pear
125g fresh pineapple
100g canned pineapple in juice
2 plums
200g papaya
100g pomegranate seeds
200g raspberries
200g strawberries

100g fresh tomato salsa
50g tzatziki
1 level tbsp orange marmalade
1 level tbsp mango chutney
1 level tsp taramasalata
1 level tbsp honey

2cm slice (about 20g) ciabatta
50g cooked puy lentils, green lentils
1 x measure (25ml) spirits (light or dark, e.g. rum, vodka)

1 tbsp single cream
1 tbsp half-fat crème fraiche
10g Parmesan
30g soft French goat's cheese
25g (1½ tbsp) light soft cheese
150ml orange juice (not from concentrate)
100ml regular soy milk
100g low-fat natural yoghurt
50g (about 3 wafer thin slices) of ham, turkey or chicken

75 CALORIES PER SERVING

150ml semi-skimmed milk
100g low-fat cottage cheese
25g (small wedge) Camembert
1 tbsp double cream
1 tbsp crème fraiche
50g ricotta cheese
¼ 125g ball of fresh mozzarella

¼ average avocado (35g)
50g smoked salmon
1 rasher back bacon, grilled or dry-fried
50g cooked, skinless chicken breast
100g cooked jumbo prawns (about 9)

1 medium apple
125g blueberries
25g dried mango

2 cream crackers
20g rice cakes (2 or 3)
20g plain breadsticks (about 4)
½ English muffin
1 slice medium white or brown bread
15g shop-bought (not takeaway) prawn crackers
1 oatcake

40g sun-dried (or sun-blush) tomatoes in oil, drained
30g (2 tbsp) raisins
1 medium egg, boiled

100 CALORIES PER SERVING

1 large egg
40g feta cheese
100g plain cottage cheese
50g (2½ tbsp) soured cream
25g blue cheese
100ml fresh custard
25g cooking chorizo
30g ready-to-eat chorizo
    (about 5 thin slices)
25g salami (about 5 thin
    slices)
1 heaped tbsp pesto

45g Parma ham
    (about 3 slices)
30g smoked mackerel fillet
1 small banana

1 level tbsp peanut butter
1 tbsp extra virgin olive oil
30g popping corn kernels
20g unsalted plain cashews
20g tortilla chips
25g wasabi peas
20g plain crisps

1 slice of thick-cut bread
½ plain bagel
1 x 45g soft white bread roll
½ regular pitta bread
1 slice German-style rye bread
1 crumpet
120g baked beans
45g dried couscous
30g dried wholewheat pasta
25g dried soba noodles
30g dried quinoa

125ml wine (white, red, rosé)
125ml sparkling wine/
    Champagne
½ pint lager
½ pint bitter
½ pint dry cider

150 CALORIES PER SERVING

35g Cheddar cheese
100g skinless chicken breast,
    baked or grilled

100g cooked brown rice
115g cooked easy-cook white
    rice
40g dried basmati rice
1 potato, baked, boiled or
    mashed without fat
    (195g raw weight)
130g baked sweet potato
    (about ½ large potato)
40g dried rice noodles
50g dried egg noodles
100g cooked pasta
40g porridge oats
50g shop-bought naan bread
    (about ½)

25g unsalted almonds
175ml wine (not sparkling)

'FREE' SAUCES

Brown sauce, in moderation;
    each tbsp is 24 calories
Fish sauce (nam pla)
Ketchup, in moderation;
    each tbsp is 20 calories
Horseradish sauce
Hot sauce (Tabasco)
Mint sauce (not jelly)
Mustard, any variety (English,
    Dijon, wholegrain,
    American)
Soy sauce
Vinegars (balsamic, white
    wine, malt, etc.)
Worcestershire sauce

Any herbs or spices

'FREE' VEGETABLES

Artichokes, including tinned
    hearts (but not in oil)
Asparagus
Aubergine
Baby sweetcorn
Beans, any green (not baked)
    (French, runner, etc.)
Bean sprouts
Beetroot, fresh, cooked
    or pickled
Broccoli
Brussels sprouts
Butternut squash
Cabbage, all kinds
    (Savoy, red, white)
Carrots
Cauliflower
Celeriac
Celery
Chicory
Chillies, including pickled
    jalapeños
Cornichons
Courgettes
Cucumber
Fennel
Garlic
Kale
Leeks
Lemons
Limes
Lettuce and salad greens
    (watercress, baby
    spinach, romaine)
Mangetout
Marrow
Mushrooms
Onions
Peppers
Pickled onions
Radishes
Shallots
Spring onions
Sugarsnap peas
Swede
Tomatoes, including tinned
    (but not sun-dried)
Turnips

simple snacks

Keep away from sweets, biscuits and crisps and try these healthier snacks instead. As tempting as sweet and savoury treats are, it's much better to reduce the amount you eat or cut them out altogether when you want to lose weight and keep it off.

100g strawberries, 27 cals

1 small pear (about 115g), 41 cals

100g seedless green grapes, 60 cals

60g hummus, 112 cals

small can tuna in brine – (80g can, 56g drained weight), 55 cals

75g raspberries, 19 cals

30g pitted green olives in brine, 31 cals

2 rye crispbreads, 62 cals

50g smoked salmon, 71 cals

50g sliced cooked ham, 54 cals

30g dried apricots, 56 cals

25g raisins, 68 cals

75g blueberries, 41 cals

1 orange (about 230g), 60 cals

1 small banana (about 155g), 96 cals

2 clementines, 44 cals

1 medium hard-boiled egg, 88 cals

1 round rice cake, 39 cals

25g mixed nuts (cashews, walnuts, almonds, pecan and hazlenuts), 145 cals

½ medium avocado, 150 cals

1 small apple (about 130g), 55 cals

2 Jaffa Cakes, 98 cals

100g peeled carrot sticks, 35 cals

20g piece of mature Cheddar cheese, 83 cals

100g skinless cooked chicken breast (roasted), 153 cals

75g cherry tomatoes, 14 cals

nutritional information
per serving

page 14 / serves 5
slow-roast chicken

213 energy (kcal)
892 energy (kJ)
34.2 protein (g)
0 carbohydrate (g)
8.4 fat (g)
2.1 saturated fat (g)
0 fibre (g)
0 sugars (g)

page 16 / serves 4
easy italian chicken

241 energy (kcal)
1020 energy (kJ)
38.6 protein (g)
8.6 carbohydrate (g)
6.1 fat (g)
1.1 saturated fat (g)
0.6 fibre (g)
7.1 sugars (g)

page 18 / serves 6
coronation chicken

449 energy (kcal)
1872 energy (kJ)
31.9 protein (g)
15.1 carbohydrate (g)
29.4 g
5.7 saturated fat (g)
1.2 fibre (g)
14.1 sugars (g)

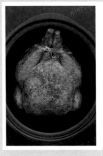

page 20 / serves 4
chinese chicken

305 energy (kcal)
1294 energy (kJ)
32.9 protein (g)
38.1 carbohydrate (g)
3.4 fat (g)
0.7 saturated fat (g)
4.1 fibre (g)
29.4 sugars (g)

page 22 / serves 4
country chicken casserole

535 energy (kcal)
2254 energy (kJ)
44.5 protein (g)
61.2 carbohydrate (g)
10.4 fat (g)
2.2 saturated fat (g)
14.4 fibre (g)
22.8 sugars (g)

page 24 / serves 4
orange and ginger chicken

228 energy (kcal)
966 energy (kJ)
36.4 protein (g)
15.4 carbohydrate (g)
2.7 fat (g)
0.6 saturated fat (g)
0.2 fibre (g)
13.1 sugars (g)

page 26 / serves 4
chicken with sticky barbecue sauce

210 energy (kcal)
890 energy (kJ)
36.6 protein (g)
12.5 carbohydrate (g)
1.8 fat (g)
0.5 saturated fat (g)
0.3 fibre (g)
12.2 sugars (g)

page 28 / serves 4
easy chicken with ham and broccoli

252 energy (kcal)
1061 energy (kJ)
42.1 protein (g)
7.6 carbohydrate (g)
5.2 fat (g)
1.0 saturated fat (g)
2.7 fibre (g)
2.1 sugars (g)

page 30 / serves 4
coq au vin

353 energy (kcal)
1487 energy (kJ)
43.3 protein (g)
14.7 carbohydrate (g)
9.4 fat (g)
2.2 saturated fat (g)
4.5 fibre (g)
8.5 sugars (g)

page 32 / serves 4
easy slow cooker curry

298 energy (kcal)
1247 energy (kJ)
32.0 protein (g)
15.3 carbohydrate (g)
12.4 fat (g)
3.6 saturated fat (g)
1.9 fibre (g)
7.9 sugars (g)

page 34 / serves 4
slow chicken pho

406 energy (kcal)
1701 energy (kJ)
38.7 protein (g)
40.2 carbohydrate (g)
9.4 fat (g)
2.6 saturated fat (g)
2.9 fibre (g)
3.3 sugars (g)

page 36 / serves 4
barley chicken and mushroom risotto

347 energy (kcal)
1465 energy (kJ)
31.8 protein (g)
36.4 carbohydrate (g)
7.7 fat (g)
1.5 saturated fat (g)
1.8 fibre (g)
2.5 sugars (g)

page 40 / serves 5
no hurry lamb curry

504 energy (kcal)
2108 energy (kJ)
40.7 protein (g)
26.8 carbohydrate (g)
27.1 fat (g)
10.8 saturated fat (g)
3.9 fibre (g)
8.0 sugars (g)

page 42 / serves 6
slow-cooked lamb with pomegranate

235 energy (kcal)
984 energy (kJ)
28.3 protein (g)
5.0 carbohydrate (g)
10.8 fat (g)
4.7 saturated fat (g)
1.0 fibre (g)
3.4 sugars (g)

page 44 / serves 4
minted lamb koftas

238/25* energy (kcal)
992/106* energy (kJ)
22.2/2.4* protein (g)
3.6/ 3.8* carbohydrate (g)
15.1/0.1* fat (g)
7.1/0* saturated fat (g)
0.8/0.3* fibre (g)
2.3/3.4* sugars (g)
*yoghurt sauce

page 46 / serves 4
garrie's lamb hot pot

518 energy (kcal)
2164 energy (kJ)
35.7 protein (g)
4.4 carbohydrate (g)
23.6 fat (g)
10.0 saturated fat (g)
8.7 fibre (g)
14.2 sugars (g)

page 48 / serves 6
lamb tagine with sweet potatoes

429 energy (kcal)
1798 energy (kJ)
31.9 protein (g)
29.6 carbohydrate (g)
21.4 fat (g)
8.9 saturated fat (g)
6.0 fibre (g)
13.5 sugars (g)

page 50 / serves 4
lamb provençal

337 energy (kcal)
1412 energy (kJ)
33.3 protein (g)
20.8 carbohydrate (g)
11.6 fat (g)
4.7 saturated fat (g)
5.4 fibre (g)
13.9 sugars (g)

page 52 / serves 6
minted slow-roast lamb

365 energy (kcal)
1522 energy (kJ)
32.4 protein (g)
7.8 carbohydrate (g)
21.7 fat (g)
9.1 saturated fat (g)
0.5 fibre (g)
5.3 sugars (g)

page 56 / serves 4
slow teriyaki beef

367 energy (kcal)
1541 energy (kJ)
38.3 protein (g)
20.3 carbohydrate (g)
15.4 fat (g)
6.7 saturated fat (g)
2.0 fibre (g)
14.3 sugars (g)

page 58 / serves 5
bolognese pasta pot

403 energy (kcal)
1699 energy (kJ)
28.4 protein (g)
46.3 carbohydrate (g)
9.8 fat (g)
3.9 saturated fat (g)
2.5 fibre (g)
6.3 sugars (g)

page 60 / serves 6
italian beef with orange

362 energy (kcal)
1519 energy (kJ)
46.3 protein (g)
13.1 carbohydrate (g)
11.8 fat (g)
4.8 saturated fat (g)
2.6 fibre (g)
8.5 sugars (g)

page 62 / serves 6
beef pot roast

360 energy (kcal)
1511 energy (kJ)
49.6 protein (g)
13.7 carbohydrate (g)
10.2 fat (g)
3.4 saturated fat (g)
4.7 fibre (g)
11.4 sugars (g)

page 64 / serves 6
beef bourguignon

468 energy (kcal)
1956 energy (kJ)
46.5 protein (g)
11.8 carbohydrate (g)
23.7 fat (g)
9.0 saturated fat (g)
2.9 fibre (g)
5.8 sugars (g)

page 66 / serves 5
beef and mushroom puff pie

495 energy (kcal)
2068 energy (kJ)
35.7protein (g)
26.5 carbohydrate (g)
26.5 fat (g)
11.6 saturated fat (g)
3.5 fibre (g)
5.1 sugars (g)

page 68 / serves 6
hungarian beef goulash

331 energy (kcal)
1392 energy (kJ)
35.9 protein (g)
17.9 carbohydrate (g)
13.6 fat (g)
5.8 saturated fat (g)
4.8 fibre (g)
13 sugars (g)

page 70 / serves 6
beef and ale stew

341 energy (kcal)
1430 energy (kJ)
34.3 protein (g)
17.4 carbohydrate (g)
13.4 fat (g)
5.8 saturated fat (g)
3.6 fibre (g)
10.7 sugars (g)

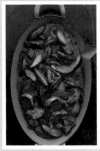

page 72 / serves 6
chunky beef chilli

405 energy (kcal)
1703 energy (kJ)
41.9 protein (g)
24.5 carbohydrate (g)
15.2 fat (g)
6.5 saturated fat (g)
8.3 fibre (g)
9.1 sugars (g)

page 76 / serves 6
classic pulled pork

342 energy (kcal)
1441 energy (kJ)
24.2 protein (g)
35.4 carbohydrate (g)
12.6 fat (g)
4.1 saturated fat (g)
2.8 fibre (g)
8.7 sugars (g)

page 78 / serves 6
mexican pulled pork tacos

337/119* energy (kcal)
1404/493* energy (kJ)
20.7/1.3* protein (g)
21.9/3.9* carbohydrate (g)
18.4/11.1* fat (g)
4.4/3.2* saturated fat (g)
2.0/2.1* fibre (g)
6.0/3.6* sugars (g)
*crunchy coleslaw

page 80 / serves 3
somerset pork and apples

379 energy (kcal)
1592 energy (kJ)
37.3 protein (g)
20.4 carbohydrate (g)
14.7 fat (g)
5.4 saturated fat (g)
2.5 fibre (g)
14.2 sugars (g)

page 82 / serves 4
sausage casserole

417 energy (kcal)
1746 energy (kJ)
26.6 protein (g)
35.9 carbohydrate (g)
19.4 fat (g)
6.5 saturated fat (g)
12.7 fibre (g)
15.7 sugars (g)

page 84 / serves 16
honey roast ham

120 energy (kcal)
501 energy (kJ)
13.3 protein (g)
0.8 carbohydrate (g)
7.1 fat (g)
2.3 saturated fat (g)
0 fibre (g)
0.8 sugars (g)

page 86 / serves 4
sticky pork ribs

488 energy (kcal)
2041 energy (kJ)
42.8 protein (g)
12.2 carbohydrate (g)
30.2 fat (g)
11.7 saturated fat (g)
0.3 fibre (g)
11.8 sugars (g)

page 88 / serves 12
pulled ham

138/202* energy (kcal)
574/840* energy (kJ)
15.7/16.3* protein (g)
0/4.8* carbohydrate (g)
8.3/13.2* fat (g)
2.8/3.3* saturated fat (g)
0/1.6* fibre (g)
0/4.8* sugars (g)
*ham and egg salad
(serves 4)

page 90 / serves 4
crustless quiche lorraine

222 energy (kcal)
923 energy (kJ)
15.1 protein (g)
7.2 carbohydrate (g)
14.9 fat (g)
5.1 saturated fat (g)
0.9 fibre (g)
3.0 sugars (g)

page 92 / serves 4
spicy pork pilaf

526 energy (kcal)
2204 energy (kJ)
29.6 protein (g)
40.8 carbohydrate (g)
28.0 fat (g)
8.6 saturated fat (g)
3.3 fibre (g)
7.0 sugars (g)

page 96 / serves 4
vegetable frittata

203 energy (kcal)
848 energy (kJ)
12.6 protein (g)
10.2 carbohydrate (g)
12.8 fat (g)
3.2 saturated fat (g)
2.6 fibre (g)
5.0 sugars (g)

page 98 / serves 4
sweet potato and root vegetable hot pot

398 energy (kcal)
1689 energy (kJ)
11.0 protein (g)
81.3 carbohydrate (g)
5.5 fat (g)
0.8 saturated fat (g)
20.3 fibre (g)
30.4 sugars (g)

page 100 / serves 4
veggie bean chilli

233/179* energy (kcal)
983/763* energy (kJ)
12.0/5.7* protein (g)
33.1/39.7* carbohydrate (g)
4.8/0.8* fat (g)
0.5/0.3* saturated fat (g)
11.1/2.1* fibre (g)
12.5/2.5* sugars (g)
*yoghurt flatbreads

page 102 / serves 4
chickpea and bean masala

234 energy (kcal)
982 energy (kJ)
11.9 protein (g)
33.7 carbohydrate (g)
5.7 fat (g)
0.7 saturated fat (g)
12.2 fibre (g)
12.7 sugars (g)

page 104 / serves 4
paneer and vegetable curry

388 energy (kcal)
1621 energy (kJ)
19.9 protein (g)
34.9 carbohydrate (g)
19.4 fat (g)
10.8 saturated fat (g)
6.8 fibre (g)
9.5 sugars (g)

page 106 / serves 4
sicilian aubergine and bean stew

216 energy (kcal)
906 energy (kJ)
8.1 protein (g)
31.5 carbohydrate (g)
5.9 fat (g)
0.7 saturated fat (g)
6.0 fibre (g)
20.0 sugars (g)

page 108 / serves 6
slow veggie bolognese

215 energy (kcal)
906 energy (kJ)
14.1 protein (g)
35.6 carbohydrate (g)
1.5 fat (g)
0.2 saturated fat (g)
9.0 fibre (g)
9.7 sugars (g)

page 110 / serves 4
sweet potato dhal

308 energy (kcal)
1306 energy (kJ)
14.0 protein (g)
58.0 carbohydrate (g)
3.9 fat (g)
0.6 saturated fat (g)
8.0 fibre (g)
10.6 sugars (g)

page 112 / serves 4
slow squash risotto

317 energy (kcal)
1338 energy (kJ)
10.7 protein (g)
49.2 carbohydrate (g)
7.7 fat (g)
2.9 saturated fat (g)
5.6 fibre (g)
11.3 sugars (g)

page 116 / serves 2
easy fish with chorizo

463 energy (kcal)
1943 energy (kJ)
44.4 protein (g)
34.1 carbohydrate (g)
16.7 fat (g)
3.8 saturated fat (g)
12.1 fibre (g)
13.3 sugars (g)

page 118 / serves 4
paella

473 energy (kcal)
1990 energy (kJ)
52.9 protein (g)
40.3 carbohydrate (g)
11.5 fat (g)
3.0 saturated fat (g)
4.1 fibre (g)
7.5 sugars (g)

page 120 / serves 4
hearty fish stew

214 energy (kcal)
899 energy (kJ)
22.3 protein (g)
20.6 carbohydrate (g)
4.3 fat (g)
0.5 saturated fat (g)
5.1 fibre (g)
6.6 sugars (g)

page 122 / serves 6
lemon and parsley salmon

372 energy (kcal)
1551 energy (kJ)
35.0 protein (g)
7.8 carbohydrate (g)
22.5 fat (g)
4.7 saturated fat (g)
1.1 fibre (g)
2.2 sugars (g)

page 124 / serves 4
chunky monkfish curry

248 energy (kcal)
1043 energy (kJ)
22.6 protein (g)
11.6 carbohydrate (g)
12.6 fat (g)
7.4 saturated fat (g)
5.2 fibre (g)
9.7 sugars (g)

page 128 / serves 6
creamy rice pudding

125 energy (kcal)
530 energy (kJ)
3.9 protein (g)
21.4 carbohydrate (g)
2.9 fat (g)
1.8 saturated fat (g)
0.2 fibre (g)
8.3 sugars (g)

page 130 / serves 4
glam porridge/sour cherry/tropical

121/190/259 energy (kcal)
509/799/1093 energy (kJ)
6.1/7.0/8.3 protein (g)
15.8/28.2/37.9 carb (g)
3.5/5.1/8.6 fat (g)
1.4/2.5/4.4 sat fat (g)
1.7/2.4/4.5 fibre (g)
5.5/15.7/26.2 sugars (g)

page 132 / serves 4
poached rhubarb with vanilla

34 energy (kcal)
148 energy (kJ)
0.9 protein (g)
8.1 carbohydrate (g)
0.1 fat (g)
0 saturated fat (g)
1.9 fibre (g)
7.4 sugars (g)

page 134 / serves 4
no-fuss crème caramel

243 energy (kcal)
1023 energy (kJ)
9.2 protein (g)
29.8 carbohydrate (g)
10.5 fat (g)
3.5 saturated fat (g)
0 fibre (g)
29.8 sugars (g)

page 136 / serves 6
apple syrup sponge pudding

229 energy (kcal)
963 energy (kJ)
5.2 protein (g)
31.5 carbohydrate (g)
10.2 fat (g)
5.4 saturated fat (g)
1.9 fibre (g)
16.0 sugars (g)

page 138 / serves 4
maple and pecan baked apples

211 energy (kcal)
884 energy (kJ)
2.0 protein (g)
36.1 carbohydrate (g)
7.4 fat (g)
0.6 saturated fat (g)
5.0 fibre (g)
35.7 sugars (g)

page 140 / serves 16
light farmhouse cake

179 energy (kcal)
755 energy (kJ)
3.4 protein (g)
27.7 carbohydrate (g)
7.0 fat (g)
3.8 saturated fat (g)
1.8 fibre (g)
18.1 sugars (g)

page 142 / serves 6
squidgy chocolate puddings

346 energy (kcal)
1449 energy (kJ)
8.4 protein (g)
39.9 carbohydrate (g)
18.1 fat (g)
10.0 saturated fat (g)
1.7 fibre (g)
20.8 sugars (g)

page 144 / serves 16
st clement's cake

159 energy (kcal)
665 energy (kJ)
5.9 protein (g)
13.3 carbohydrate (g)
9.5 fat (g)
1.2 saturated fat (g)
0.6 fibre (g)
10.6 sugars (g)

page 146 / serves 6
plum and apple crunch

99 energy (kcal)
421 energy (kJ)
0.8 protein (g)
25.0 carbohydrate (g)
0.2 fat (g)
0 saturated fat (g)
3.7 fibre (g)
25.0 sugars (g)

page 150 / serves 6
mixed root soup

139 energy (kcal)
584 energy (kJ)
2.7 protein (g)
26.7 carbohydrate (g)
3.1 fat (g)
0.5 saturated fat (g)
7.8 fibre (g)
14.2 sugars (g)

page 152 / serves 6
celeriac soup

72 energy (kcal)
296 energy (kJ)
3.1 protein (g)
8.2 carbohydrate (g)
3.1 fat (g)
0.4 saturated fat (g)
7.8 fibre (g)
6.1 sugars (g)

page 154 / serves 6
french-style yoghurt

76 energy (kcal)
316 energy (kJ)
4.0 protein (g)
5.5 carbohydrate (g)
4.3 fat (g)
2.7 saturated fat (g)
0 fibre (g)
5.5 sugars (g)

page 156 / serves 4
jacket potatoes

186 energy (kcal)
787 energy (kJ)
4.6 protein (g)
39.8 carbohydrate (g)
2.0 fat (g)
0.2 saturated fat (g)
4.0 fibre (g)
1.4 sugars (g)

page 158 / serves 4
loaded sweet potatoes

379 energy (kcal)
1603 energy (kJ)
10.5 protein (g)
65.2 carbohydrate (g)
10.4 fat (g)
5.3 saturated fat (g)
10.9 fibre (g)
18.2 sugars (g)

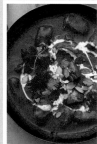

page 160 / serves 12
basic korma sauce

99 energy (kcal)
412 energy (kJ)
2.0 protein (g)
12.1 carbohydrate (g)
5.0 fat (g)
2.0 saturated fat (g)
2.3 fibre (g)
7.8 sugars (g)

page 160 / serves 4
chicken korma/prawn korma

325/171 energy (kcal)
1361/713 energy (kJ)
38.9/17.5 protein (g)
12.5/12.4 carbohydrate (g)
13.5/ 5.9 fat (g)
4.2/2.2 saturated fat (g)
2.7/2.3 fibre (g)
8.0/7.8 sugars (g)

page 162 / serves 12
basic balti sauce

109 energy (kcal)
457 energy (kJ)
2.9 protein (g)
14.8 carbohydrate (g)
4.7 fat (g)
0.4 saturated fat (g)
2.9 fibre (g)
10.5 sugars (g)

page 162 / serves 4
balti chicken

315 energy (kcal)
1326 energy (kJ)
39.7 protein (g)
19.2 carbohydrate (g)
9.3 fat (g)
1.3 saturated fat (g)
4.6 fibre (g)
14.7 sugars (g)

page 164 / serves 8
basic bolognese

270 energy (kcal)
1135 energy (kJ)
28.4 protein (g)
14.3 carbohydrate (g)
10.3 fat (g)
4.3 saturated fat (g)
3.3 fibre (g)
6.2 sugars (g)

page 166 / serves 10
simple tomato pasta sauce

55 energy (kcal)
230 energy (kJ)
1.6 protein (g)
7.3 carbohydrate (g)
2.4 fat (g)
0.3 saturated fat (g)
1.9 fibre (g)
5.6 sugars (g)

page 168 / makes 1.3 litres
chicken stock

25 energy (kcal)
104 energy (kJ)
3.2 protein (g)
1.8 carbohydrate (g)
0.4 fat (g)
0.1 saturated fat (g)
0.5 fibre (g)
0.5 sugars (g)
per 100ml

page 170 / makes 1.25 litres
beef bone broth

28 energy (kcal)
118 energy (kJ)
4.2 protein (g)
2.2 carbohydrate (g)
0.1 fat (g)
0 saturated fat (g)
0.6 fibre (g)
0.9 sugars (g)
per 100ml

index

a

almonds, flaked: coronation chicken 19

almonds, ground: St Clement's cake 145

apples, cooking: maple and pecan
baked apples 138

apples, eating
apple syrup sponge pudding 137
plum and apple crunch 146
Somerset pork and apples 80

aubergines: Sicilian aubergine and
bean stew 107

b

bacon
beef bourguignon 64
coq au vin 31
crustless quiche lorraine 91
loaded sweet potatoes 158
quick gravy 14

baked beans: sausage casserole 83

bananas: tropical fruit porridge 131

beansprouts: chicken pho 35

beef
basic Bolognese sauce 164
beef and ale stew 70
beef and mushroom puff pie 66
beef bone broth 171
beef bourguignon 64
beef curry 32
beef pot roast 63
Bolognese pasta pot 58
chunky beef chilli 73
Hungarian beef goulash 69
Italian beef with orange 61

slow teriyaki beef 56

bread
classic pulled pork 76
yoghurt flatbreads 101

breadcrumbs
squidgy chocolate puddings 142
stuffing for fish 122

broccoli
chicken pho 35
chicken with ham and broccoli 28
loaded sweet potatoes 158

butterbeans
lamb provençal 50
sweet potato and root vegetable
hotpot 98

butternut squash risotto 113

c

cabbage: crunchy coleslaw 79

cannellini beans: Sicilian aubergine
and bean stew 107

carrots
beef and ale stew 70
beef bone broth 171
beef pot roast 63
chicken stock 168
chickpea and bean masala 102
country chicken casserole 23
crunchy coleslaw 79
lamb hot pot 46
mixed root soup 150
sweet potato and root vegetable
hotpot 98
veggie Bolognese 108

celeriac soup 153

Cheddar

   crustless quiche lorraine 91

   loaded sweet potatoes 158

cheese

   crustless quiche lorraine 91

   loaded sweet potatoes 158

   paneer and vegetable curry 104

   squash risotto 113

cherries, dried: sour cherry and

   cinnamon porridge 131

chicken

   balti chicken 163

   barley chicken and mushroom

    risotto 36

   chicken curry 32

   chicken korma 160

   chicken pho 35

   chicken stock 168

   chicken with ham and broccoli 28

   chicken with sticky barbecue sauce 27

   Chinese chicken 20

   coq au vin 31

   coronation chicken 19

   country chicken casserole 23

   Italian chicken 16

   orange and ginger chicken 24

   paella 119

   roast chicken 14

chickpeas

   chickpea and bean

    masala 102

   fish with chorizo 116

   lamb tagine with sweet potatoes 49

chocolate

   sour cherry and cinnamon

    porridge 131

   squidgy chocolate puddings 142

chorizo

   fish with chorizo 116

paella 119

   spicy pork pilaf 92

cider

   country chicken casserole 23

   Somerset pork and apples 80

cocoa powder: squidgy chocolate

   puddings 142

coconut

   monkfish curry 124

   tropical fruit porridge 131

corn tacos: Mexican pulled pork

   tacos 79

courgettes

   fish with chorizo 116

   lamb provençal 50

   veggie Bolognese 108

cream, double: korma sauce 160

cream, soured

   crunchy coleslaw 79

   loaded sweet potatoes 158

crème fraiche

   loaded sweet potatoes 158

   sour cherry and cinnamon porridge 131

cucumber

   ham and egg salad 89

   minted cucumber and yoghurt

    sauce 45

e

eggs

   apple syrup sponge pudding 137

   crème caramel 134

   crustless quiche lorraine 91

   ham and egg salad 89

   light farmhouse cake 140

   St Clement's cake 145

   squidgy chocolate puddings 142

   vegetable frittata 96

f

fennel: fish stew 120

fish

    fish stew 120

    fish with chorizo 116

    lemon and parsley salmon 122

    monkfish curry 124

g

Grana Padano: squash

    risotto 113

green beans

    paella 119

    spicy pork pilaf 92

Gruyère: crustless quiche lorraine 91

h

ham

    ham and egg salad 89

    honey roast ham 84

    pulled ham 89

ham, smoked: easy chicken with ham

    and broccoli 28

l

lamb

    lamb curries 32, 40

    lamb hot pot 46

    lamb provençal 50

    lamb tagine with sweet potatoes 49

    lamb with pomegranate 42

    minted lamb koftas 45

    minted roast lamb 53

leeks: crustless quiche lorraine 91

lemons

    apple syrup sponge pudding 137

    lemon and parsley salmon 122

    lemon syrup 145

    maple and pecan baked apples 138

    minted lamb koftas 45

    St Clement's cake 145

lettuce

    classic pulled pork 76

    ham and egg salad 89

    Mexican pulled pork tacos 79

m

mango, dried: tropical fruit porridge 131

maple syrup

    maple and pecan baked apples 138

    maple crunch 146

marinades: Mexican 79

mayonnaise

    coronation chicken 19

    crunchy coleslaw 79

milk, full-fat: French-style yoghurt 154

milk, semi-skimmed

    apple syrup sponge pudding 137

    celeriac soup 153

    creamy rice pudding 128

    crème caramel 134

    crustless quiche lorraine 91

    glam porridge 131

    sour cherry and cinnamon

        porridge 131

    squidgy chocolate puddings 142

    tropical fruit porridge 131

    vegetable frittata 96

mixed beans

    chickpea and bean masala 102

    veggie bean chilli 101

mixed dried fruit

    light farmhouse cake 140

    maple and pecan baked apples 138

    see also sultanas

monkfish curry 124

mushrooms
  barley chicken and mushroom risotto 36
  basic Bolognese 164
  beef and mushroom puff pie 66
  beef bourguignon 64
  Bolognese pasta pot 58
  coq au vin 31
  veggie Bolognese 108

n
noodles, rice: chicken pho 35

o
olives: Italian chicken 16
orange marmalade: orange and ginger
  chicken 24
oranges
  Italian beef with orange 61
  light farmhouse cake 140
  St Clement's cake 145

p
paneer and vegetable curry 104
papaya, dried: tropical fruit porridge 131
Parmesan: squash risotto 113
parsnips
  country chicken casserole 23
  mixed root soup 150
  sweet potato and root vegetable
    hotpot 98
pasta: Bolognese pasta pot 58
pastry: beef and mushroom puff pie 66
pearl barley: barley chicken and
  mushroom risotto 36
peas
  country chicken casserole 23
  lamb hot pot 46

paneer and vegetable curry 104
vegetable frittata 96
pecan nuts: maple and pecan baked
  apples 138
peppers
  balti chicken 163
  Chinese chicken 20
  fish with chorizo 116
  Hungarian beef goulash 69
  lamb provençal 50
  monkfish curry 124
  paella 119
  spicy pork pilaf 92
  vegetable frittata 96
  veggie Bolognese 108
pine nuts: Sicilian aubergine and
  bean stew 107
pineapple: Chinese chicken 20
pineapple, dried: tropical fruit
  porridge 131
plum and apple crunch 146
pomegranates: lamb with
  pomegranate 42
pork
  classic pulled pork 76
  Mexican pulled pork tacos 79
  sausage casserole 83
  Somerset pork and apples 80
  spicy pork pilaf 92
  sticky pork ribs 86
  see also bacon; ham
porridge oats
  glam porridge 131
  maple crunch 146
  sour cherry and cinnamon porridge 131
  tropical fruit porridge 131
potatoes
  country chicken casserole 23
  fish stew 120
  jacket potatoes 157

lamb hot pot 46
    paneer and vegetable curry 104
prawns
    paella 119
    prawn korma 160
prunes: light farmhouse cake 140
puff pastry: beef and mushroom puff pie 66
Puy lentils: veggie bolognese 108

r
red kidney beans
    chunky beef chilli 73
    sausage casserole 83
    veggie bean chilli 101
red lentils
    basic Bolognese 164
    lamb curry 40
    sweet potato dhal 110
    veggie Bolognese 108
rhubarb: poached rhubarb with
    vanilla 132
rice, long-grain: spicy pork pilaf 92
rice, short-grain
    creamy rice pudding 128
    paella 119
    slow baked squash risotto 113
rice noodles: chicken pho 35

s
salad cream: ham and egg salad 89
salmon: lemon and parsley salmon 122
sausage casserole 83
sauces
    balti sauce 163
    basic Bolognese sauce 164
    korma sauce 160
    mint sauce 53
    quick gravy 14
    sticky barbecue sauce 27
    tomato pasta sauce 166
seafood: paella 119
shallots
    chicken with ham and broccoli 28
    coq au vin 31
    golden spiced shallots 110
shellfish
    paella 119
    prawn korma 160
slow cooking principles 8–11
soups
    celeriac soup 153
    mixed root soup 150
spinach
    chickpea and bean masala 102
    paneer and vegetable curry 104
    squash risotto 113
squid: paella 119
strawberries: low-sugar strawberry
    jam 128
sultanas
    coronation chicken 19
    teriyaki beef 56
see also mixed dried fruit
sweet potatoes
    lamb tagine with sweet potatoes 49
    loaded sweet potatoes 158
    mixed root soup 150
    sweet potato and root vegetable
    hotpot 98
    sweet potato dhal 110

t
tomato pasta sauce 166
    easy Italian chicken 16
tomatoes
    balti sauce 163
    basic Bolognese 164

Bolognese pasta pot 58
chickpea and bean masala 102
chunky beef chilli 73
classic pulled pork 76
coq au vin 31
fish stew 120
fish with chorizo 116
ham and egg salad 89
Hungarian beef goulash 69
Italian beef with orange 61
lamb curry 40
lamb provençal 50
lamb tagine with sweet potatoes 49
monkfish curry 124
paneer and vegetable curry 104
sausage casserole 83
Sicilian aubergine and bean stew 107
sweet potato and root vegetable
    hotpot 98

tomato pasta sauce 166
veggie bean chilli 101
veggie bolognese 108

w
water chestnuts: Chinese chicken 20
white fish
    fish stew 120
    fish with chorizo 116

y
yoghurt
    coronation chicken 19
    French-style yoghurt 154
    minted cucumber and yoghurt sauce 45
    tropical fruit porridge 131
    yoghurt flatbreads 101

First published in Great Britain in 2016
by Orion Publishing Group Ltd
Carmelite House
50 Victoria Embankment
London, EC4Y 0DZ
An Hachette UK Company

10 9 8 7 6 5 4 3 2 1

A CIP catalogue record for this book is available
from the British Library.

ISBN: 978 1 4091 5475 4

Designer: Smith & Gilmour
Photographer: Cristian Barnett
Project manager: Claire Bignell
Creative director: Justine Pattison
Nutritional analysis calculated by: Lauren Brignell
Recipe assistants: Emma Webber, Rebecca Roberts
Kitchen assistant: Alice Cleary
Project editor: Jillian Young
Copy editor: Elise See Tai
Proofreaders: Liz Jones and Mary-Jane Wilkins
Indexer: Rosemary Dear

Printed and bound in China

MIX
Paper from
responsible sources
FSC® C015829
FSC
www.fsc.org

Acknowledgements

Firstly, huge thanks to everyone who enjoys my recipes
and the way I cook. You have given me such fantastic
feedback; I hope you like these dishes just as much.

An enormous thank you to my family, John, Jess and
Emily, for your input and enthusiasm for my slow
cooked recipes – however many times you tried them.

I'm truly grateful to the very talented photographer
Cristian Barnett for wonderful photographs that really
make my food come to life. And the brilliant Claire
Bignell for her superb organisational and creative skills,
selecting the perfect props and helping to make the
recipes look both beautiful and achievable.

Massive thanks to Lauren Brignell for all her invaluable
nutritional support and the hundreds of recipes she has
analysed over the past few months. Also, thanks to
Emma Webber and Rebecca Roberts for testing the
recipes and assisting on shoot days. And not forgetting
the wonderful Tamsin Mann and Mary Holder for
helping with last minute work in the test kitchen – and
dashing to the supermarket at a moment's notice.

At Orion, I would like to thank Amanda Harris for
believing in this project right from the beginning and
for trusting me to get on and develop the series. Also
Elizabeth Bond, for her continued support for *Without
the Calories* – I appreciate your commitment to these
books. Also thank you to Jillian Young, my fantastic
editor, for her guidance and the meticulous Lucy
Haenlein for taking over the project and seeing it
through to publication. Mark McGinlay for managing
the PR side of things so smoothly and Helen Ewing for
her design input.

I'm also grateful to my agent, Zoe King, at The Blair
Partnership, for her constant encouragement and
enthusiasm, the legal team at TBP for handling the
business side of things and Jo Hayes for her dedication.
And many thanks John Basset for all your help and
advice.

A final thank you to my family and my friends for their
unwavering support.